Michelle Morgan

Madonna

ROBINSON

RUNNING PRESS
PHILADELPHIA · LONDON

ROBINSON

First published in Great Britain in 2015 by
Robinson

Copyright © Michelle Morgan, 2015

The moral right of the author has been asserted.

A CIP catalogue record for this book
is available from the British Library.

ISBN 978-1-47211-886-8 (paperback)
ISBN: 978-1-47211-943-8 (ebook)

Design by Andrew Barron
Typeset in FF Din
Printed and bound in China by
C&C Joint Printing Co.

Robinson
is an imprint of
Constable & Robinson Ltd
100 Victoria Embankment
London EC4Y 0DY

An Hachette UK Company
www.hachette.co.uk

www.constablerobinson.com

First published in the United States in 2015 by
Running Press Book Publishers,
A Member of the Perseus Books Group

Books published by Running Press are available
at special discounts for bulk purchases in the
United States by corporations, institutions, and
other organizations. For more information,
please contact the Special Markets Department
at the Perseus Books Group, 2300 Chestnut
Street, Suite 200, Philadelphia, PA 19103, or
call (800) 810-4145, ext. 5000, or email special.
markets@perseusbooks.com.

US ISBN: 978-0-7624-5621-5
US Library of Congress Control Number:
2014943004

9 8 7 6 5 4 3 2 1

Digit on the right indicates the number
of this printing

Running Press Book Publishers
2300 Chestnut Street
Philadelphia, PA 19103-4371

Visit us on the web!
www.runningpress.com

This book is dedicated to Madonna.

And to Tara Hanks, Fraser Penney and Paul Maggs, who all love her as much as I do.

Acknowledgements

I would like to thank everyone who has encouraged my love of Madonna over the past thirty years, especially my friends, Claire, Helen, Mandy, Loraine, Katharine and Sharon. I have bombarded you with more information than I'm sure you ever wanted to know, and I very much appreciate your patience and good humour!

To Mum, Dad, Paul, Wendy and Angelina – I knew the only way you would ever have a Madonna book in your collection was if I wrote one, so here it is; your first ever piece of memorabilia. May it be the first of many!

To my agent, Robert Smith, and my publishers, Constable & Robinson/ Little, Brown and Running Press.

I'd especially like to thank Duncan Proudfoot for seeing the potential in this project, and Allie Collins for her editing.

To Peter Kentes, for allowing me the use of his beautiful photo of Madonna, which he took while they were both students at the University of Michigan.

To my husband, Richard, who has come to appreciate Madonna over the past twenty-seven years, has accompanied me to many of her concerts and thoroughly admires her work ethic. He has sat through all of her movies, and even drove me thirty miles just so I could watch *Evita* on the big screen. I am forever grateful to him for everything he does for me and for our family.

To my daughter, Daisy, who has listened to Madonna since she was in my tummy and whose song will always be the 2003 track "Nothing Fails". She may not appreciate Madonna's music (yet!) but she loves *The English Roses* book and greatly admires her work in Africa, as well as the adoption of two children.

Finally, I'd like to thank my readers for supporting my career, and being so enthusiastic about this book. I appreciate you more than you will ever know.

Picture credits

© Getty Images
Pages 21, 23, 25, 27, 29, 31, 33, 35, 55, 67, 71, 73, 77, 89, 117, 123, 129, 135, 197, 205, 265, 281, 283, 342, 363, 383, 409, 421, 423, 433, 441.

© Peter Kentes
Page 19.

© Rex Features
Pages 9, 11, 13, 15, 17, 37, 39, 41, 43, 45, 47, 49, 51, 53, 57, 59, 61, 63, 65, 69, 75, 79, 81, 83, 85, 87, 91, 93, 95, 97, 99, 101, 103, 105, 107, 109, 111, 113, 115, 119, 121, 125, 127, 131, 133, 137, 139, 141, 143, 145, 147, 149, 151, 153, 155, 157, 159, 161, 163, 165, 167, 169, 171, 173, 175, 177, 179, 181, 183, 185, 187, 189. 191, 193, 195, 199, 201, 203, 207, 209, 211, 213, 215, 217, 219, 221, 223, 225, 227, 229, 231,233, 235, 237, 239, 241, 243, 245, 247, 249, 251, 253, 255, 257, 259, 261, 263, 267, 269, 271, 273, 275, 277, 279, 285, 287, 289, 291, 293, 295, 297, 299, 301, 303, 305, 307, 309, 311, 313, 315, 317, 319, 321, 323, 325, 327, 329, 331, 333, 335, 337, 339, 341, 345, 347, 349, 351, 353, 355, 357, 359, 361, 365, 367, 369,371, 373, 375, 377, 379, 381, 385, 387, 389, 391, 393, 395, 397, 399, 401, 403, 405, 407, 411, 413, 415, 417, 419, 425, 427, 429, 431, 435, 437, 439, 443, 445, 447, 448.

Introduction

The thirteenth of December 1984: a pretty nondescript day in England. It was certainly cold, possibly icy, and I was probably wondering what to buy my friends and family for Christmas. That evening I was in my bedroom, getting ready to go to Thursday club; a youth club of sorts which was held at my school, and the highlight of my week. I was fourteen years old and as my parents disliked *Top of the Pops* immensely, I was watching it upstairs on my old black-and-white television. Downstairs our Betamax video was taping the programme, so that I could finally watch it the next day in colour.

As I applied my twilight-teaser lipstick and dusted off my ra-ra skirt, a young woman came onto the screen and sang "Like a Virgin". She had long, straight hair and was wearing cut-off trousers and a belted jacket. I didn't know who she was, but I knew she was someone important. When they flashed up her name – Madonna – at the end of the song, I was sure it wouldn't be the last time I saw this funky, self-assured woman.

The next day I watched the clip again but this time in colour, and realised that Madonna's hair was not blonde as it had looked in black-and-white, but bright pink. It was a wig, but wearing such an outrageous (for the time) look on a national TV show just confirmed my thoughts that she was a force to be reckoned with.

After that moment, my posters of Wham! and Duran Duran were replaced by pictures of the bangle-wearing, midriff-showing singer. She became my idol, and I'd be a liar if I said I never dressed up as her. I did, of course, with varying degrees of success. My cut-off tops and leggings were fairly popular, but my yellow nail varnish and blue lipstick caused my parents to comment that I looked like I had some kind of exotic disease. However, while I may have wanted to be just like Madonna on occasions, more than anything she became a role model; someone to inspire me and reinforce the idea that dreams really do come true.

I have seen Madonna in concert six times, and have collected every magazine cover, book, album and DVD I can find. I have yet to meet the woman herself, but seeing her vast list of accomplishments over the past thirty years has given me great encouragement to go after my own dreams of becoming a full-time writer. This is something that finally happened several years ago, after many years of hard work and sheer bloody-mindedness.

Within my desire to become a writer was the dream to do a book about Madonna, but not a salacious, tell-all biography, which I know she has particular distaste for. Instead, I wanted to put together a tribute which fans around the world could appreciate; and what better way to do that than to create an illustrated volume, telling her story through a series of photos and extended captions. I am ecstatic, therefore, to present to you a book – a celebration, if you will – made up of 220 iconic or interesting moments of Madonna's life and career. It is written from the heart, with photos chosen by myself, and I very much hope that you will all enjoy reading it as much as I enjoyed putting it together.

See? I told you dreams come true, didn't I?

Michelle Morgan, June 2014

Born into an Italian-American Catholic family, Madonna Louise Veronica Ciccone (she chose the name Veronica herself, during her confirmation) came into the world on 16 August 1958. She was the eldest daughter of six children, and was named after her mother, Madonna Fortin. For the first five years, her life in Michigan was one of relative (if slightly chaotic) ease, until her mother was diagnosed with breast cancer in the early 1960s. The young child did not understand what was going on, and Madonna later revealed how she remembers begging her mother to play while her mum cried silently, unable to summon the energy to do anything.

Finally, after a long battle with the disease, Madonna Senior passed away and the family were devastated. Madonna would later say that she thought it a fitting tribute that she was named after her mother, who was destined to die very young. She has also described her as the most perfect woman and mother who ever lived.

This photo shows Madonna as a toddler (wearing a striped blouse) with family and friends, a few years before her mother's death.

The young Madonna missed her mother terribly, and from that moment on made a decision that she would never be hurt by anyone or anything ever again. She was extremely angry that her mother had been taken away, and later remembered that when neighbours came to the house to see how everyone was, it would just make her even more upset, and she couldn't wait for them to leave so that she could grieve in private.

After the family had recovered as much as they could, the young girl threw herself into school work, looked after her brothers and sisters, and very much became the woman of the house. Her father adored her, and the attention she received ultimately caused conflict between her and her siblings. A great sense of competition began in order to see who could gain the most attention from their father, and it seemed Madonna was always the winner. Because of this, her brothers would often pick on her; at one point apparently pinning her to the washing line by her underwear.

This photo shows Madonna after her mother's death, on stage during a dance performance. She is the brunette child on the right.

After Madonna Senior's death, housekeepers were a frequent but unwanted presence in the Ciccone household, and the children did their best to chase each and every one away. Finally, Joan Gustafson joined the family, and before long a relationship began between Joan and Madonna's father, Sylvio (Tony). When it was announced in 1966 that the two were to marry, the children did not take kindly to the news. Madonna later remembered that her father wanted everyone to call Joan "Mom", but the young child struggled to get the words out of her mouth. From that moment on, she resented the woman who she felt had taken her place in her father's affections, and became deeply unhappy with the situation.

The children became further frustrated when Joan gave birth to two more siblings – Mario and Jennifer – stretching the family income even further with two new mouths to feed. The tension between Joan and Madonna continued for some years, but since becoming a mother herself, the singer seems to have mellowed towards her step-mother, declaring that she was probably unfair in her treatment of her whilst growing up.

This photo shows Tony and Joan, with their children, Mario and Jennifer.

As Madonna became a teenager, she took great interest in the subject of dance. She began attending lessons with a teacher called Christopher Flynn, who was to become a major influence in her life. Flynn saw something very special in his young student and encouraged her love of dance, taking her to gay nightclubs and introducing her to things that her strict Catholic upbringing had never let her be privy to in the past.

During this time, Madonna was asked by a high-school friend if she would like to take part in his amateur film, to be recorded on his Super 8 camera. She said yes, and was filmed on the sundeck of a house she was babysitting in at the time, eating a raw egg and then having one "fried" on her stomach by an obliging female friend. Once cooked, the girl then ate the egg from Madonna's stomach using a knife and fork. The film was very much just high-school fun, but it is interesting, nevertheless, and has been shown in several documentaries over the years.

This photo shows Madonna in a garden, around the time she was taking dance lessons with Flynn.

In spite of this photo showing Madonna in the company of male friend Brian Campbell, she has made no secret of the fact that in high school she wasn't particularly popular with boys. Choosing not to shave her legs or underarms, and rarely bothering with make-up, the teenage Madonna seems to have been far more concerned with her dance lessons than with anything boys had to offer.

The fact that she refused to perform any kind of personal grooming would often lead to her being teased by other students, and she would return home crying and upset. Madonna later said that her father tried to get her to understand that if she was going out of her way to be different, then she should accept that there would be people eager to knock her down a peg or two. This was to be a good lesson learned for the future.

During this time, Madonna joined her high-school cheerleading troupe, and spent many hours rehearsing after class. The hobby complemented her dance training well, and was also a good way of getting out of babysitting duties at home. One teacher later remembered that, while Madonna's step-mother frequently wanted her home by a particular time, staff would phone to explain that she would need to stay late in order to practise her cheerleading. This enabled the teenager to skip off to a dance class without her parents complaining that she was late returning to the house.

Madonna

After graduating from high school, Madonna enrolled at the University of Michigan, where she shared an apartment with two young men and a woman called Whitley Setrakian. Whitley would later remember that, while she was initially intimidated by Madonna, generally their time together was a happy one. The two obtained jobs at an ice-cream store to pay for their dance classes, and spent their free time going to parties and nightclubs around town. Still, no matter how late the evening was, Madonna would always be up and out to class by 8 a.m., such was her devotion to her studies.

The dancer was a popular student, making friends with a young musician called Stephen Bray and even visiting nightclubs with her teachers. By this time Christopher Flynn was teaching at the university, and he continually encouraged her to move to New York and follow her dreams. While she was hesitant at first, after one year on campus she decided that in order to become a professional dancer, she would need to move to the city. Her family did not want her to go, but in spite of that, Madonna packed her bags and boarded a plane to her future.

Madonna chose to leave Michigan and head to New York with only $35 in her pocket and no approval or permission from her father. By the time she arrived, the future singer ended up in a seedy apartment, with drug dealers in the hallways and shady characters lurking in the shadows. She began dance lessons with Pearl Lang, and spent so much time dressed in leotards and ripped tights that it prompted other people in the building to mistake her for a prostitute. This was something she could later laugh about, but certainly did not appreciate at the time.

Meanwhile, her father would travel to New York on a regular basis, begging Madonna to come home. She would assure him that all was well and that he had no reason to worry, and send him on his way. The visits would upset her, however, due mainly to the fact that she felt so lonely and isolated in the large city, with no real friends to call her own. During the 1998 documentary *Madonna Rising*, the star told Rupert Everett that she would get very sad during her first years in New York. "I used to cry and cry and cry and long for familiarity," she said. It should also be noted that Madonna later revealed to *Harper's Bazaar* that she had been sexually assaulted by a stranger on the street shortly after arriving in New York, which can only have added to her desperation and unhappiness. However, in spite of the loneliness, Madonna was determined never to return to Detroit, instead wanting more than ever to make a name for herself in New York.

In order to support her dance studies, Madonna took odd jobs as a hat-check girl at the Russian Tea Room and a "jelly squirter" filling doughnuts at Dunkin' Donuts. Neither job paid much money, and she later laughed that the reason she was fired from Dunkin' Donuts was because she squirted the jelly too liberally – mainly all over the equipment rather than the food.

She discovered that photography students at the New School were looking for models, and what's more, they were also offering a lot more money than she ever earned in regular jobs. After that, when not dancing, the twenty-year-old Madonna would head to the school and pose for three hours (often nude) to earn enough money to buy food. Dinner would be yoghurt, nuts and occasionally popcorn, depending on how much money she had earned that week.

Sometimes Madonna was offered private work at photographers' studios (aka their dingy apartments), but as long as it was above board, she didn't mind. "It was really good money and very flexible hours which is why I chose to do it – it wasn't because I enjoyed taking my clothes off," she told Rupert Everett during the 1998 television special *Madonna Rising*.

When it was clear that dancing would not earn her a good living, Madonna began going to auditions for a variety of different entertainment jobs. At one point she found herself auditioning to be a backing singer for French disco artist Patrick Hernandez, which brought her to the attention of two French producers. Telling her she could be a big star, the two men flew Madonna to Paris, put her up in a posh apartment, gave her a car and a driver, and paid her so much money she didn't know what to do with it all.

The singer was there for six months in total, during which time she did a little work and a lot of thinking, and eventually she decided that, while singing was definitely what she wanted to do with her life, she did not wish to be moulded into the producers' idea of what a star should be. Madonna told the men that she would be going back to America for a holiday, but she never returned to Paris. Instead, she set herself up in New York and put everything she had into learning to write music in order to begin a career that was controlled by herself, not by anyone else. "I wanted to earn it," she later said.

In 1979, Madonna saw an advert looking for actors to star in a low-budget film entitled *A Certain Sacrifice*, which was being made in New York. She wrote a long, personal letter to writer/director Stephen Jon Lewicki, who was so intrigued by her unusual approach that he agreed to give her an audition. The role was an unpaid one, but Madonna insisted she be given $100 for her services. Lewicki complied, but insisted she sign a release. She did and eventually won the role of Bruna, a passionate "bad girl" who lives with a group of love-slaves but falls in love with a relatively "normal" young man.

The film was not exactly well acted, nor did it make for pleasant viewing, and at one point it includes some rather disturbing scenes after Bruna is raped by a man in a restaurant toilet. After recovering physically, she decides to take revenge on her attacker, and together with her friends and lovers she drives around New York in order to find him. Eventually they do track him down and Bruna and friends end up carrying out a sacrifice, complete with tomato-ketchup blood and an awful lot of dramatics.

A Certain Sacrifice required Madonna to disrobe and take part in scenes that at the time were described as "soft porn". By today's standards it is all relatively tame, but in spite of that, she was not thrilled when the film was eventually released in 1985. She tried to block it; not for the nude scenes, she insisted, but because it was horribly acted. The singer lost the case due to the fact that she had signed a release form, and the film went to video, selling thousands of copies around the world.

The film wasn't the only time Madonna appeared before a camera during her journey to stardom. After *A Certain Sacrifice*, she landed a role in a Curt Royston project entitled *In Artificial Light*, which consisted of various individual pieces all written by the actors themselves. During her section, Madonna recites her own poetry, talks about her philosophies and is filmed performing a song called "Hot House Flower" with her band. It didn't catapult her to stardom, but it did leave a better impression than *A Certain Sacrifice*.

This photo and the one on the previous page are both from the series of pictures that Madonna would send to prospective producers when looking for work.

When Madonna began her journey into music, she enlisted the help of various friends, including then-boyfriend Dan Gilroy and, later, university friend Stephen Bray. She also set up several bands, most notably the Breakfast Club and Emmy, which gave her experience of writing songs, playing the drums and guitar, as well as organising gigs. However, not happy with being hidden behind a drum kit all evening, Madonna eventually persuaded the other band members to let her sing a few songs. Having tasted the limelight, it wasn't long before she was anxious not to be part of a band at all, but to exist as an artist on her own.

Squatting in several apartments, including a synagogue with Gilroy and New York's infamous Music Building, Madonna still lived a lonely life, which was made worse when one of her apartments was broken into and the thieves made off with her music equipment. She also had a failed business relationship with a management company, owing mainly to the fact that they wanted her to concentrate on rock-and-roll music, while she was very much about making good pop songs.

During the early years there were times when she was homeless, living on friends' sofas and occasionally searching through trash cans for food. Hers was no *X Factor* rise to fame, and there were no Svengalis to make everything work out well. But no matter how bad her life was, Madonna worked furiously on her music every single day, believing that one day she would become a fully fledged star and be able to leave all the troubled times behind her.

After her various failed attempts at stardom, Madonna put together an audition tape and took it around every New York DJ she could find, hoping that they would play it in their clubs. She eventually found someone who was willing to do it, and was thrilled when people flocked to the dance floor whenever it was played. From this moment, the singer began to be noticed, and finally gained a circle of friends who not only took away her blues, but also made life more interesting.

One of the DJs Madonna became friends with was Mark Kamins, who was so impressed with her work that he arranged for her to meet Sire Records executive Michael Rosenblatt. A short time later the singer found herself in a hospital room occupied by Seymour Stein, President of Sire Records, who had been told about her by Rosenblatt. Stein later joked that Madonna would not have minded if he was lying in a coffin, as long as his arm was out and he was able to sign the deal. Armed with her boom box and tape, which included the song "Everybody", Madonna played her music to Stein and he was so impressed that he signed her immediately.

After signing to Sire, Madonna wasted
no time getting into the studio. Her
first album, released in July 1983 and
called simply *Madonna*, was a roaring
success, and included five singles:
"Lucky Star", "Borderline", "Burning
Up", "Holiday" and "Everybody". The
tracks were all very much pop songs,
and "Holiday" has gone onto become
one of the most famous Madonna
songs of all time, performed frequently
and re-released three times in the UK,
entering the top ten every time.

All of the singles released from
the first album had official videos,
except "Holiday" which is generally
showcased using an appearance
from the television show *Solid Gold*.
"Borderline" was Madonna's first
story video, and told the tale of a girl
and boy in a fairly toxic relationship,
which is pushed to the limits when she
is discovered by a photographer on
the street. "Lucky Star", meanwhile,
featured Madonna dancing and singing
while showing off her famous belly
button.

This publicity photo shows
Madonna's early style, including her
graffiti tag, "Boy Toy".

Once Madonna began to release music, her career started to hot up very quickly – although this didn't stop her being rejected when she tried out for a part in the television series *Fame*. Auditioning for the role of Danny's girlfriend, the singer was deemed too tough for the part. She didn't have much time to mourn, however, as she embarked on a series of publicity events, interviews and appearances. Among these was a spot on *American Bandstand*, where she told host Dick Clark that she wanted to rule the world. She also enjoyed a trip to the UK to appear on television shows *The Tube* and *Top of the Pops*.

Madonna's early interviews and appearances are extremely interesting to watch, due mainly to the fact that she was young and hungry to achieve something wonderful in her life. But in spite of the fact that she was just starting out, her confidence was soaring. In one memorable interview for a programme called *Ear Say*, she takes the film crew around New York, including a trip into the subway, where she talks about an upcoming tour, film and album. "Sometimes," she said, "people think that if you're a girl you're gonna be a pushover and they can get away with more – pull the wool over your eyes – but I just surprise them and they see that they're wrong."

The first of Madonna's boyfriends to really make the news was music producer John "Jellybean" Benitez, whom she dated just as her star began to rise. The two were introduced when she was making music with the Breakfast Club, and once they began going out, it was a match made in music heaven.

The two were off and on as a couple for a few years, and during that time they worked together on various songs. For instance, when Madonna was unhappy with some of the tracks on her first album, Jellybean took them and, in his words, "sweetened them up" by adding guitars and extra vocals. She repaid the favour when she wrote a song for him entitled "Sidewalk Talk" and even contributed some of the vocals for the track, helping it to reach number one in various charts around the USA.

While the two enjoyed a relationship for a while, it does not appear to have been extremely serious on Madonna's part. When asked by reporters at the time if the two were contemplating marriage, she became very agitated and asked why they should. They parted ways soon afterwards, romantically at least.

This photo shows Madonna, Jellybean (in Mickey Mouse T-shirt) and friends, at a New York party in 1983.

Out of all the MTV award ceremonies Madonna has attended, one of the most famous was in September 1984, when she appeared on stage wearing a wedding dress. Perched on top of a wedding cake complete with fake groom, the singer made her way down the prop while singing her new single, "Like a Virgin". By the time she reached the bottom, her hair was loose, her shoes had been kicked off and she was rolling around on the floor.

The performance caused a huge stir, not least for Madonna's manager, who was backstage declaring her career was over before it had begun. Later the singer said that the reason she ended up on the floor was because she was trying to retrieve her shoes. It is true that Madonna can be seen putting her shoes back on, but by the end, when she is rolling around at the front of the stage and exposing her underwear to the audience, her shoes are firmly on her feet.

As it turned out, the performance was not the beginning of the end for Madonna; in fact, if anything, her place in pop music history was cemented from that moment on.

Released in November 1984, Madonna's next album, *Like a Virgin*, had been delayed thanks to the continued popularity of her first album, and in particular the single "Borderline". During recording, she enlisted the help of old friend Stephen Bray to write some of the songs, and he – along with Nile Rodgers and Madonna herself – also helped to produce the record. The singer was frustrated that the album was delayed, but by the time it did come out, fans flocked to record shops and it shot straight to the top of the charts. With nine new songs, including "Material Girl", "Angel", "Dress You Up" and the title track, the album was a fabulous success, with a cover showing Madonna in a wedding dress, hair curly and wild, with a sultry look on her face.

In 1985, after the release of the film *Desperately Seeking Susan*, which Madonna starred in and which featured her song "Into the Groove", the track was released as a single and added to the album (and later the CD), making the earlier vinyl edition a much-valued item in any Madonna fan's collection.

This photo shows Madonna posing for a publicity photo during the *Like a Virgin* era.

In January 1985, Madonna appeared at the American Music Awards with singer Huey Lewis, in order to present the award for best black album. "I want them all to win," she exclaimed before reading out the nominations for albums by Lionel Richie, Prince and Michael Jackson. The winner was *Purple Rain* by Prince, and he made his way to the stage not only with his backing singers, but with his huge bodyguard too.

While Prince may not have spoken to Madonna (or to anyone) when he accepted his award, the two did apparently go on a few dates, though she soon became tired of his approach to life. For instance, Madonna disliked his insistence on having bodyguards wherever he went, and then in 1994 she told an interviewer that during one meeting "he was just sipping tea, very daintily. I have a theory about people who don't eat. They annoy me." Madonna became agitated and the two quickly went their separate ways, though they did reunite briefly for the 1989 track "Love Song", for the *Like A Prayer* album.

This photo shows Madonna posing for photographers during the night of the awards.

A movie made in 1983, but not released until 1985, was *Vision Quest* (aka *Crazy for You*), starring Matthew Modine and Linda Fiorentino. The coming-of-age story has been all but forgotten in cinema history, but it remains famous in Madonna circles, purely for the fact that the star appears as a nightclub singer in two scenes.

The part came about when Madonna was spotted by filmmakers (including music producer Phil Ramone) singing in New York, and they loved her look so much that they snapped her up for the film. She was ecstatic and declared it an extremely important role because it introduced her to the world not only as a singer, but as a performer and actress too. The part enabled Madonna to belt out hits such as the revved-up "Gambler" and the beautiful ballad "Crazy for You" in a setting very similar to the one she had been used to performing in shortly before becoming famous.

The two singles used in the movie were released during the course of 1985 and went onto become big hits, though they have only ever been performed publicly on several occasions; "Crazy for You" during *The Virgin* and *Re-invention* tours, and "Gambler" during *The Virgin Tour* only.

"Material Girl" was the second single released from the *Like a Virgin* album, and if nothing else, has succeeded in giving Madonna a moniker used time and time again in the media. The song tells the story of a woman hell-bent on having as many luxuries as she can possibly obtain, as she lives her life in the material world.

The video for the song was heavily inspired by the Marilyn Monroe film *Gentlemen Prefer Blondes*, and in particular the "Diamonds are a Girl's Best Friend" number. Madonna was seen dressed in a pink gown identical to Marilyn's, and danced across the set with a number of young men in tow all eager to supply her with an array of gems and furs. The flipside of the video came during the acted-out "off-set" moments, showing Madonna giving away such luxuries in favour of a man promising wilted flowers and a trip in a beat-up truck.

The "Material Girl" video has gone down in history as one of Madonna's most classic clips, and has become legendary thanks to the story that young actor Sean Penn met Madonna on the set and asked her out. She apparently spurned his advances, but later agreed to go out with him – to eat hotdogs at the famous Pinks stand in Los Angeles.

Back in the days when Madonna was a struggling singer, she was spotted sitting on her apartment stoop by a photographer whose mother was a casting agent. One thing led to another, and before she knew it, she was asked to audition for a part in a film called *Desperately Seeking Susan*. She was successful and the film went on to become one of the most famous of her career.

The story revolves around unhappy housewife Roberta (played by Rosanna Arquette) who is obsessed with reading the adventures of Susan (Madonna) in the New York personal ads. She becomes so embroiled in her life that it isn't long before Roberta is travelling into the city in order to spy on Susan's comings and goings. One thing leads to another, and after an accident she ends up losing her memory and being mistaken for Susan, thereby creating an adventure of her own. By the end the situation is rectified, and Roberta not only finds her own identity, but her true love as well.

The film was officially a vehicle for co-star Arquette, but when it was released in March 1985, Madonna stole the show due to her new-found fame and notoriety. People also sat up and listened when it was revealed that she had provided a song entitled "Into the Groove", which was featured in the movie as well as the soundtrack.

This photo shows Madonna and Rosanna in a publicity still for the movie.

The triumph of Madonna's first two albums sent her on the road for *The Virgin Tour*, which saw the singer playing packed venues around the United States.

The concert itself was a mixture of hits from the first and second albums, along with "Gambler" and "Crazy for You", from the *Vision Quest* movie. With the help of two backing dancers/singers, Madonna danced throughout the concert, and even rolled around during "Like a Virgin", in exactly the way she had at the infamous MTV awards.

The unofficial rule of being in attendance at one of the gigs was that you had to dress as much like Madonna as you possibly could. The result of this was that when Madonna took to the stage, all she could see were hundreds of women looking just like her. So alike were the audience, in fact, that rumour has it Madonna would often go out and mingle with the crowd before performances, and she was seen as just another lookalike at each and every one.

At the end of each concert on the tour, just as she finished a rendition of "Material Girl", Madonna was seen stripping off her jewellery while a voice pretending to be her father was heard over the loud-speaker. "Come down from the stage this instant," he tells her. "But Daddy, I'm having a good time," Madonna replies. This had been a joke during the entire tour, but by the time they reached Detroit, her real-life dad was in the audience, and he happily got up on stage to play out the scene for real. Laughingly seen being dragged off stage, the singer then announced that she was not leaving without her fur, and raced back on to retrieve it. The crowd went crazy. Afterwards, Madonna jokingly told reporters that her dad actually hurt her arm as he pulled her from the stage, such was his enthusiasm for the part.

The Detroit fans enjoyed seeing the singer's family in the crowd, and also appreciated hearing her talk about how much it meant to be back in the city. Describing how she had never been seen as a "Homecoming Queen", Madonna then told the audience that she certainly felt like one at that moment, before appearing to burst into tears.

This photo shows Madonna at *The Virgin Tour* after-show party, in June 1985.

Live Aid, one of the biggest rock concerts ever organised, took place in London and Philadelphia on 13 July 1985 and included almost every star on the planet, including Queen, U2 and David Bowie. At the time, Madonna was reeling from the publication of nude photos from her student days in *Penthouse* and *Playboy*, and many predicted that the singer would not perform because of it. However, in true Madonna style, she declared she was not ashamed, and travelled to the Philadelphia gig with new fiancé Sean Penn.

Describing her as "the woman who pulled herself up by her bra straps, and has been known to let them down occasionally", Bette Midler introduced Madonna, who danced on to the stage as if she didn't have a care in the world. Wearing flowery trousers, a cut-off shirt and long jacket, Madonna sang "Holiday", "Into the Groove" and "Love Makes the World go Round" while laughing off chants of "Take off your coat!" from the audience. "I ain't taking shit off today!" she squealed. "You might hold it against me ten years from now!"

The wedding of the year, 1985 – that of Madonna and actor Sean Penn – took place on 16 August in a mountain-top garden in Malibu. Reporters were seen hiding in the bushes and trying to bluff their way into the house – and when that failed, they hired helicopters in order to fly overhead. By the time the bride appeared in the garden dressed in a huge white dress with a black bowler hat and veil, there were over a dozen copters buzzing in the sky.

"That whole time was almost too much," Madonna revealed, and declared the entire affair "a circus".

She later saw the funny side, but Sean Penn became so incensed with the unwanted attention that he was apparently seen running around on the beach below the house, writing provocative messages for the reporters in the sand. Despite the noise, the wedding itself was actually rather civilised, with a Catholic priest marrying the couple in a traditional ceremony. Madonna vowed to stay with her husband "till death do we part", but did not, it should be said, promise to obey.

A dramatic change of image came for Madonna in early 1986, when she released the single "Live to Tell". The first track from her forthcoming *True Blue* album, the song was used as the soundtrack for Sean Penn's film *At Close Range*, in which he starred with Christopher Walken and Mary Stuart Masterson. The video for the ballad showed Madonna with Marilyn Monroe-style hair, a simple flowered dress and minimal make-up.

It was quite a surprise for the many fans that had come to know Madonna as the girl who wore umpteen rubber bracelets and back-combed her hair. Of the change of image, Madonna said that she just felt the need to get rid of everything and start over again. "I had to be cleaned thoroughly," she explained. This would be the start of many changes of image that soon gained her the nickname "the Queen of Re-invention".

This photo shows Madonna during the making of *Shanghai Surprise*, in which she sported the same hair style and image that she had earlier premiered in the "Live to Tell" video.

When Madonna and Sean Penn decided to team up to make *Shanghai Surprise* – a movie in which they played a missionary and a fortune-hunting tie salesman respectively – it should have been a perfect match. Unfortunately, it proved to be the opposite, and during the filming in Hong Kong, the two actors were said to have fought consistently. Madonna later denied this, however, and said that actually the couple had felt as though it was them against the world. They quickly became aloof with other cast members and when the production landed in England, the newspapers christened them "The Poison Penns", a nickname that stayed with them for so long that apparently Madonna started signing their Christmas cards that way.

The film's producer, ex-Beatle George Harrison, was highly disappointed by the bad press and encouraged Madonna to take part in a press conference, which only seemed to fuel the fire of negativity surrounding the film. This was not Madonna's fault, however, as the questions that day were not only intrusive, but predictably geared towards getting a reaction out of the already-stressed star. It is fair to say that she did not rise to the bait, and footage shows her acting with calm and resilience in a very hostile environment.

This photo shows Madonna and Sean in a scene from *Shanghai Surprise*.

While *Shanghai Surprise* was anything but easy to film, and the London stopover was something of a disaster, Madonna was able to have at least a little bit of light relief when she visited the Joseph Tricot fashion show on a rare day off. Dressed casually in a black top and denim jacket, the singer piled her hair behind her head and wore her glasses for a better view. Unfortunately this outing was not enough to keep her mood sunny for long, and after the London stay, it was consistently reported that the singer and her husband were involved in various bust-ups and fall-outs. "Madonna's Marriage On Rocks" screamed a headline in the *People*, while the *News of the World* asked, "Madonna and Sean: Are they really the Poison Penns?"

Once the movie was released, the reviews were predictably poor. Madonna responded to the backlash by saying, "That's a pity because I like the film a lot," before adding that she would just have to chalk it up to experience. While *Shanghai Surprise* is certainly not one of her best, it must be said that she had probably never looked more beautiful or vulnerable as she did in this particular screen role.

This photo shows Madonna at the fashion show she attended during her day off in London.

In June 1986, Madonna released her new album, *True Blue*, which provided the world with the singles "Live to Tell", "Open Your Heart", "La Isla Bonita", "True Blue" and "Papa Don't Preach". All were big hits, but perhaps the ones that created the most controversy were "Papa Don't Preach" and "Open Your Heart", thanks to the videos released with them.

In the latter video, the singer introduced her now-famous pointy bra, and was seen cavorting as a stripper in a seedy peep show before dancing down the street with a young friend, played by actor Felix Howard. There were complaints from parents that the video was inappropriate for a younger audience, but they were even more concerned with the promo for "Papa Don't Preach". The song and video revolved around the story of a young girl (played by Madonna), who

becomes pregnant by her mechanic boyfriend (played by Alex McArthur). The teenager is determined to keep the baby, and the video shows her dancing with her boyfriend, hanging out with friends, worrying about her situation and finally breaking the news to her concerned father, played by actor Danny Aiello.

The video, in which Madonna sported a very short hairstyle, a leather jacket and a T-shirt with the words "Italians Do It Better" emblazoned across the front, angered various women's groups, who claimed that it was the singer's own papa that should be preaching. While the song and video were certainly not to everyone's taste, there is no doubt that it has gone down in history as one of her classics, and is still occasionally played on MTV and radio, nearly thirty years later.

Madonna's next song from the *True Blue* album was the title track, which offered a whole new perspective to the one seen in "Papa Don't Preach". There were no controversies, no storylines that could offend right-wing groups, and instead it was just a wonderful, old-fashioned pop song, obviously inspired by times gone by.

The video that accompanied the song showed Madonna in leggings, an electric blue 1950s-style dress and with platinum hair, dancing with her girlfriends and pretending to drive a Ford Thunderbird convertible. If ever there was a happy Madonna video, this has to be it.

The song itself was inspired by Sean Penn, and the album was also dedicated to him, calling the actor "the coolest guy in the universe". Because of this, "True Blue" has only been performed during one tour: *Who's That Girl* in 1987.

This photograph shows Madonna dancing in the video.

Madonna

In August 1986, Madonna made her professional stage debut in David Rabe's play *Goose and Tomtom*, with Sean Penn, Harvey Keitel and Barry Miller. Rehearsals took place at the Lincoln Center in New York, but strangely, up until the last minute Rabe could not decide whether or not to show it to the public.

Madonna played the part of Lorraine, a woman who teams up with two jewellery thieves, Goose (Barry Miller) and Tomtom (Sean Penn). The play was not an easy one to understand, but the rehearsals did make good fodder for the media, and photographers continually sat outside waiting for the couple to emerge with scripts in hand.

In the end, after all the rehearsals and photographs, Rabe decided on a performance in front of a very limited, invited audience, and then that was that; the play ended without any press, fanfare or regular punters at all. This made the entire project look more like a theatre workshop than a fully fledged production, and the world will never get to find out just how good it could have been.

This photo shows Madonna and Sean Penn leaving the Lincoln Center after attending rehearsals for the play.

In November 1986, Madonna showed her support for AIDS sufferers when she took part in a fundraiser fashion show at Barney's clothes store in New York. The benefit was held for the AIDS Research Clinic at St Vincent's Hospital, and the singer joined the likes of model Iman to strut her stuff on the catwalk. The designers for the jackets modelled that day were Madonna's friends Andy Warhol, Jean-Michel Basquiat and Keith Haring; all of whom would sadly go on to have early deaths.

After Jean-Michel's passing, Madonna wrote an article about their friendship, saying that he would sometimes get up at 3 a.m. in order to create his art. She also described how she wasn't surprised when he died, as he was too fragile for the world, and that one evening when she dined with Andy Warhol, Keith Haring and Jean-Michel, she felt like "the luckiest girl in the world to have known all of them".

This photo shows Madonna being hugged by Iman, as they both wear designer denim jackets at the charity event.

In late 1986, Madonna took to the streets of New York in order to make a comedy initially called *Slammer*, but renamed *Who's That Girl* out of respect for Sean Penn, who ended up in the real-life slammer at the time of its release. The film was a comedy about a young woman called Nikki Finn (played by Madonna) who is trying to clear her name of a crime she didn't commit. At the very beginning of the movie, Nikki is released from prison, and a young man called Louden Trott (Griffin Dunne) is assigned by his future father-in-law to take her straight to the bus depot. Of course, the trip doesn't go at all to plan, and before he knows it, Louden is involved in an adventure which sees him being chased by gangsters, making friends with a cougar called Murray and finally falling in love with Nikki herself.

At the time, Madonna said she was attracted to the movie because of the sweetness of her character. She also enjoyed the thought of playing a lady who was tough on the outside, but very soft and vulnerable inside; her rough exterior masking the sadness within.

This photo shows Madonna and Griffin Dunne as Nikki and Louden, together with their cougar friend Murray.

The premiere for the *Who's That Girl* movie took place in Times Square in the summer of 1987. Madonna, dressed in a stunning silver gown, stood on a platform and informed the audience that ten summers ago she had taken her first plane ride in order to travel to New York. As the fans cheered, she explained that she had asked the cab driver to drop her off in the middle of everything, and he'd taken her to Times Square. "I was completely awestruck," she told the audience, before adding that ten years later, as she stood in the very place where she had been dropped off, she once again felt completely awestruck.

Unfortunately, the critics did not feel the same way about the film, and declared it a stinker from the start. Even Madonna's cougar co-star got better reviews than she did, but while the singer later said that she had given a bad performance in a bad movie, perhaps this was a little harsh. Her fans still enjoyed it, and nearly three decades later the screwball comedy is being discovered by a whole new generation.

The *Who's That Girl* tour was the first time Madonna had embarked on an international concert, and it was an almighty accomplishment. Having sold out within minutes, the shows began in Japan and took in the USA and Europe in almost three months, with Madonna making headlines wherever she went.

Compared to future tours, *Who's That Girl* was a relatively tame affair, but at the time it seemed really quite elaborate. There were moving walkways, a bright red telephone box where Madonna got changed at one point during the show, and a multitude of costumes designed by Marlene Stewart. The show began with "Open Your Heart", featuring Madonna in a corset – complete with pointy bra – dancing with thirteen-year-old Chris Finch. From there the show went into "Lucky Star", before a costume change for "True Blue" and "Papa Don't Preach", during which she was seen wearing a pale blue 1950s-style dress.

An amusing moment in the *Who's That Girl* show came when Madonna sang a medley of "Dress You Up", "Material Girl" and "Like a Virgin", which contained probably the most elaborate of her costumes at the time – a dress covered in toys, trinkets and other paraphernalia. It was at this point that she bent over to reveal a pair of lace panties, worn over her corset, before ripping them off and throwing them into the crowd.

The last part of the concert was probably the most energetic, with "Into the Groove", "La Isla Bonita", "Who's That Girl" and "Holiday". At this point, soaked in sweat and with her hair glued to her face, Madonna would stop the show and ask people to throw their combs onto the stage. Many people did, and she would brush her bedraggled hair before continuing – and concluding – the concert.

This photo and the one on the previous page show Madonna playing at Wembley Stadium, London, in August 1987.

In August 1987 the *Who's That Girl* tour hit the UK, and the most famous singer in the world arrived to a huge crowd at Heathrow Airport. The UK leg of the tour began in Roundhay Park in Leeds, then headed to London's Wembley Stadium for several shows. Frenzied fans camped outside the singer's hotel just to catch a glimpse of her, and she didn't disappoint, with frequent shopping trips and even more regular runs, wearing dark glasses and accompanied by a team of bodyguards. Very frequently the press and fans would try to run alongside her, only to give up exhausted after a short time. Madonna, however, kept on running, oblivious it seemed to the constant shouts from admirers and the tussles between bodyguards and the paparazzi.

For the entire visit, England was abuzz with excitement; her concerts were reported on by ITN television news and newspapers were filled with gossip and photographs. Even cover-to-cover magazines appeared, charting every movement Madonna made. When she finally left, moving on to the next stop on the European leg of the tour, the country seemed to be a quieter place, with only an array of jogging wannabes pounding the pavement as a reminder that the superstar was once there.

This photo shows Madonna shopping in London in 1987 during a day off.

After a somewhat tumultuous year, during which they were separated thanks to her tour and his time in jail for punching an extra on the set of his movie *Colors*, Madonna and Sean put on a happy front and headed to a Los Angeles AIDS benefit in November 1987. They looked so relaxed in each other's company that some people took this to mean the two were now back on track. Others, meanwhile, went one further and announced that they were about to renew their wedding vows in a star-studded ceremony.

The reality was that the marriage was in deep trouble, and around Thanksgiving, not long after their appearance at the benefit, the pair called it off and divorce papers were served. Madonna's people assured the press that it was a mutual decision, based on the fact that they just weren't happy anymore. However, much to the surprise of everyone, just a few weeks later the singer had a change of heart; they reunited and the divorce was called off.

This photo shows the pair at the charity event, shortly before the impending separation was announced.

Madonna

For most people, this photo of a platinum-blonde Madonna is the image most associated with the singer during 1987. Gone were the ripped clothes of old, and in their place were the styles of Hollywood luminaries from the 1940s and 1950s. While it is true to say that personally it may have been a stressful year, professionally 1987 was a great one for the singer, and she topped it off with the release of a new album, *You Can Dance*.

The record was very much a remix project, with new samplings of old favourites such as "Holiday", "Everybody", "Into the Groove" and several others from her early albums. It also boasted one new song – "Spotlight" – which was written with old friend Stephen Bray and produced by John "Jellybean" Benitez. The album was well-received by fans, and Madonna liked the reworking of "Into the Groove" so much that she went on to use the track in her 1990 *Blond Ambition* tour.

1988 was a hard year for Madonna fans, primarily because for the first time since fame came her way, the singer was not releasing an album, a film or both. However, for those lucky enough to be in New York, this was not a hardship, because in May 1988 Madonna opened in the David Mamet play *Speed the Plow*.

Madonna played the part of Karen, a downtrodden secretary with no glamour or style to speak of. The character finds herself working for a temperamental Hollywood executive, played by Joe Mantegna, and the play revolves around her time with him and his associate, played by Ron Silver.

After the first performance, Madonna described the experience as being "like really good sex". Some years later she looked at it in a deeper way, telling interviewer Larry King that she took the part in order to gain experience, and thoroughly enjoyed being on stage as there are no second chances. "When you make a movie you get a chance to do another take. When you're on stage, you say the line wrong, that's it; it's out there, it happened."

Most critics were in agreement after the play opened, saying they disliked her performance and declaring that Madonna could not act. However, fans did not feel the same way, and tickets for each performance sold out every night.

This photo shows Madonna after the opening night performance, closely followed by long-term press rep Liz Rosenberg.

Around the time she was appearing in *Speed the Plow*, Madonna began a friendship with comedienne Sandra Bernhard. The two started hanging out together after the show, frequenting nightclubs and being photographed intensely – mainly by newspapers eager to see whether the two women were more than just good friends. They caused headlines during a colourful rendition of "I've Got You Babe" at a 1989 charity concert, but that was nothing compared to their appearance on the *Late Show with David Letterman* in 1988. Dressed identically in white T-shirts, denim shirts and white socks, their "performance" raised many eyebrows as they hinted at being intimate together and then joked that Sandra had slept with Sean Penn. "She's using me to get to Sean," Madonna laughed, though few (especially Penn, it can be imagined) thought it was funny.

The friendship with Sandra lasted only a few years, and was said to have ended after Madonna became friends with Ingrid Casares, a friend of Bernhard's whom the singer felt sorry for, after apparently being treated badly by the comedienne.

This photo shows them in the early 1990s, shortly before their friendship ended.

In August 1988, Madonna held a press conference to encourage people to attend Sport Aid's Race Against Time, an event designed to be run simultaneously in countries throughout the world. The proceeds from sponsorship were to be given to a children's charity, and during her short speech Madonna spoke passionately, telling patrons that all they needed to show support was a pair of running shoes. She also said that participation would help the world to look back on the 1980s as the era that enabled children to be free of hunger and pain. "Make a difference in a hungry child's life," she told reporters.

The press conference and her participation in the race showed that underprivileged children were very much on Madonna's radar, almost twenty years before she began working in Malawi and adopted two infants of her own.

This photo shows the singer at the conference, showing off her race registration number.

Throughout their marriage, Madonna and Sean Penn were forever rumoured to be separating and then getting back together again, and after their divorce was called off in 1987, public attention on the couple was even more extreme. Penn apparently hated the media attention they received during each outing, and Madonna did not appreciate the frequent outbursts he made towards the photographers. Seeing photos of Madonna hiding behind her handbag while Sean hurled abuse at paparazzi was a frequent event, but it all came to an end in December 1988 when the couple really did split for good. Stories vary, but it is said that during an altercation in their home, Sean abused and threatened his terrified wife to such a degree that she headed to the sheriff's office. Newspapers at the time reported that Madonna was left extremely shaken, and the *Sunday Mirror* told readers she had filed charges accusing him of "extreme brutality". Neither Sean nor Madonna ever spoke publicly about what really happened on that evening, but she did eventually drop the charges against her ex and later told several interviewers that she was just too immature to be married at that time. "I do miss it though," she poignantly admitted.

This photo shows the couple looking strained at a Mike Tyson boxing match, shortly before they separated.

Released in March 1989, *Like a Prayer* was the first album Madonna made after her divorce from Sean Penn. The record, which was dedicated to the singer's mother, was the most raw of all her albums thus far, and included tracks about her mother's death, her father, siblings and, most of all, her marriage. The album featured the singles, "Like a Prayer", "Express Yourself", "Cherish", "Oh Father", "Dear Jessie" and "Keep it Together",

and saw Madonna working with old friends Pat Leonard and Stephen Bray, as well as Prince, who co-wrote a track entitled "Love Song".

The album brought forth a more serious side to Madonna, with long, dark hair and an overall more spiritual look. It was a critical and commercial smash, and is still widely thought of as one of the most important Madonna albums ever released.

The first song released from the *Like a Prayer* album was the title track. It was a huge hit, though not without controversy, especially when the video was released. The promo featured a combination of burning crosses, an innocent man being accused of murder, and Madonna (after revealing a stigmata on her hands) kissing a black Christ-like figure in a church.

All this was too much for Pepsi, who had just signed her to appear in a two-minute video advertising their drink. The firm had paid Madonna $5 million to use the track in the commercial, but when executives saw the official video and began to receive complaints about the content, they immediately pulled the plug. Pepsi were said to be furious at the outcome, but Madonna less so. The hoo-ha ensured her album gained maximum publicity – and she reportedly got to keep the $5 million too.

While "Like a Prayer" caused a certain amount of chaos, a less controversial video came with the "Express Yourself" single. It showed a totally different side to Madonna – short blonde hair, singing about the benefits of respecting oneself. It was a positive, thought-provoking song, and the video was inspired by the Fritz Lang movie *Metropolis* (1927). When it was released, it was the most expensive music video ever made.

It was much less scandalous than "Like a Prayer", though the media did latch on to the fact that at one point Madonna wore a chain around her neck and was seen licking milk from a bowl before pouring it over her shoulder. The idea for this scene came from the director, rather than from Madonna herself, and it is extremely tame compared to modern-day music videos. However, it did become one of the most famous parts of the whole thing, along with a crotch-grabbing scene inspired – one would imagine – by another 1980s superstar, Michael Jackson.

Madonna's previous film, *Who's That Girl*, had been something of a box-office failure, and while she hoped her next movie would bring better luck, it sadly didn't earn her any more respect from the critics. Starring Matt Dillon, Jennifer Grey, Randy Quaid and a variety of other famous actors, *Bloodhounds of Broadway* revolved around four stories taking place on New Year's Eve, 1928. Madonna played Hortense Hathaway, a showgirl with an unsavoury reputation, and the object of desire for Feet Samuels, played by Quaid.

Filmed at the end of 1987, the film gave Madonna the opportunity of a duet with *Dirty Dancing* star Jennifer Grey. However, even that wasn't enough to save the movie, and when it was eventually released in November 1989, the critics were not impressed.

This photo shows Madonna as Hortense, dressed in full 1920s costume, complete with Louise Brooks-style bobbed hair.

Madonna

March 1990 saw Madonna release the single "Vogue", which was inspired by a new dance craze of the same name, along with her part in the forthcoming *Dick Tracy* movie. The video included singers from her upcoming *Blond Ambition* tour, was shot in black-and-white and took on a vibe from the Golden Age of Hollywood.

Madonna, sporting short platinum hair and several racy outfits – such as her soon-to-be-famous Gaultier cone bra, and a see-through lace blouse –

sang about such luminaries as Marilyn Monroe, Bette Davis, Jean Harlow and Marlene Dietrich, while performing "vogue" moves with her dancers.

The song was a huge hit, reaching number one in many countries, and has gone on to become one of the most famous Madonna tunes of all time. She has also performed the track live on many occasions, most recently during the 2012 Super Bowl half-time show and the *MDNA* tour.

Probably the most famous of all her tours, *Blond Ambition* saw Madonna once again travel the world, in one of the most ambitious and stylised shows that had ever been produced at the time. Beginning in April 1990 and continuing until August, the show was a masterpiece, showcasing songs such as "Open Your Heart", "Holiday", "Like a Prayer" and everything in between.

For the first time Jean Paul Gaultier was in charge of costumes, and as a result the infamous cone bra that everyone associates with Madonna was born. This piece of engineering was worn in various forms throughout the show; sometimes under a jacket, other times in the shape of a corset. But while the costumes were definitely a talking point, perhaps the most controversial moment was when the singer took to a bed in order to sing "Like a Virgin", the performance of which included a masturbation scene at the end of the song. This infamous part of the show angered many religious groups, and Madonna was even threatened with arrest whilst performing in Toronto. It also caused her a certain degree of embarrassment when she had to perform it in front of her father in Detroit.

This photo shows the singer at Wembley Stadium, modelling the infamous Jean Paul Gaultier cone bra.

The middle section of *Blond Ambition* was a tribute to the movie *Dick Tracy*, which Madonna had recently made, and this led on to the final part of the show, which included a variety of fun numbers: "Material Girl", "Cherish", "Into the Groove", "Vogue" and "Holiday". The finale – "Keep it Together" – featured the singer with all of the dancers on stage, doing a series of strategic moves with chairs before each member of the cast (and sometimes the crew too) jumped into a hole. This would then leave Madonna on her own, sitting on a chair and singing to the crowd, before finally exiting the stage.

The Blond Ambition tour has never been released on an official DVD, though parts of it were shown in the *Truth or Dare* movie.

This photo shows Madonna during the Japanese leg of her tour. By the time the show hit Europe, the ponytail extension had been replaced with the singer's natural hair in short curls.

The *Blond Ambition* tour brought Madonna and her entourage back to London for the first time since the *Who's That Girl* tour three years before. Once again she was photographed jogging around town, complete with bouncers, fans and reporters desperately trying to keep up; and yet again the media went wild, trying to report on every bit of the trip.

The London stopover saw the singer play at Wembley Stadium for several nights, including one show that was broadcast live over BBC radio. Unfortunately, someone at the corporation took it upon themselves to warn Madonna not to swear as she would be live on air; a comment that was like a red rag to a bull. The singer not only swore, but did so over and over again, prompting complaints to the BBC and a hastily released apology.

Further controversy came when the singer insisted on doing soundchecks for hours inside the stadium, while fans sat outside in blisteringly hot conditions. However, in spite of that, the audience loved the show and it gained many positive reviews in the press.

This photo shows Madonna on a rare day off, exiting a London restaurant.

Dick Tracy is a 1990 movie starring Warren Beatty and a host of other stars, including Madonna, Dustin Hoffman and Al Pacino. Madonna played Breathless Mahoney, a baddie-but-goody who enjoys a flirtation with the ever-so-good Dick Tracy, played by Beatty. The singer appears with platinum hair and a host of 1930s-style outfits, and while Stephen Sondheim was in charge of the official soundtrack, Madonna provided her own album too, in the shape of *I'm Breathless*. The album was inspired by the movie and included "Vogue" and several tracks from the film itself.

Dick Tracy was not an altogether easy movie to make, as Madonna had to sing some very complicated songs that challenged her vocal range. She was also said to have found working with Al Pacino strenuous; he played Big Boy Caprice, the main antagonist who is often seen bullying Breathless.

This photo shows the two in a happy moment, during a light-hearted publicity still.

A romance between Madonna and Warren Beatty came about while the two were working together on *Dick Tracy*. Many dismissed it as a publicity stunt, and it is true that the relationship did seem to be over very quickly, but to say it was all a gimmick is surely unfair. Despite the large age gap, Madonna and Warren seemed to get along very well, though their relationship was sorely tested while she was on tour and being filmed for the documentary *Truth or Dare* during her *Blond Ambition* world tour.

At one point during filming, the singer's voice doctor asks if she'd like to turn the camera off while they talked, to which Warren replied, "She doesn't want to live off-camera, much less talk." The actor ends his comment with a chuckle, but it seems the pressure may have been getting to him, as by the time the movie came out, the couple had split, and most of Beatty's time on screen ended up on the cutting-room floor. It is interesting to note that Madonna later laughed off his comments, claiming it to be a case of "the pot calling the kettle black".

It is doubtful that the couple stayed in regular contact after the split, and he soon became involved with Annette Bening, whom he is still married to now. However, they were in the same venue on at least one occasion afterwards, when they were photographed looking quite cordial at a party to celebrate the release of the movie *Two Girls and a Guy* in 1998.

Madonna has always been known for her amazing (and often outrageous) costumes, but perhaps the most elaborate of all was the one she wore for the 1990 MTV awards. The singer dressed as Marie Antoinette, complete with huge dress, heavy blonde wig, jewels and a fan; the latter she used as a prop throughout the song.

With the help of the *Blond Ambition* dancers and her backing singers Niki Harris and Donna DeLory, Madonna sang her single "Vogue". She also danced around a set in keeping with the theme, which featured large mirrors, imitation marble pillars, heavy curtains and a chaise longue which she lay on while being carried off stage at the end of the performance.

As with most things, the song was not without controversy, as the performance involved some of the dancers groping Madonna's chest, and another putting his head up her skirt. But in spite of that, it was very much a tongue-in-cheek look at the court of Marie Antoinette, and remains one of the most imaginative and memorable MTV performances.

Towards the end of 1990, Madonna released her first greatest hits album, entitled *The Immaculate Collection*. The CD probably wouldn't have caused much of a stir at all if it hadn't been for one of the extra tracks – a slow-tempo (almost spoken) song entitled "Justify My Love". The tune itself was fairly low-key, but once again the accompanying video sent shock waves around the world. In the black-and-white clip, Madonna is seen walking into a hotel, where she is soon gazing at a variety of sexually liberated people and taking part in a love scene with both a woman and a man (the man played by her then-boyfriend Tony Ward).

The video showed semi-nudity as well as sadomasochism, and caused such a scandal that it was banned from everywhere but obscure late-night television programmes. Eventually it was released for purchase on video, though Madonna assured fans that selling it was never her intention; she had wanted it to be played on MTV and was disappointed when it was immediately banned.

Still, the singer was able to see the funny side of the scandal when she parodied it on an episode of *Saturday Night Live*, with the help of *Wayne's World* favourites Mike Myers and Dana Carvey.

This photo shows Madonna with video co-star/boyfriend Tony Ward, just before the surrounding controversy hit the headlines.

Dick Tracy was relatively well received by critics, and while Madonna may not have won any Oscars for her performance, the movie did give her the opportunity to sing the film's theme tune, "Sooner or Later", at the 1991 Academy Awards. She attended the event with Michael Jackson as her date, and was dressed in a glamorous white gown complete with fur stole.

The performance was breathtaking, but she later complained that there were several problems, including the fact that one of her earrings started to fall from her ear and descend into her perfectly styled hair. The song and persona portrayed by Madonna onstage inspired comparisons to Marilyn Monroe, though the singer has always been quick to state that, while she is a big fan of the actress, they don't have too much in common personality-wise.

That said, she has paid homage to Marilyn on numerous occasions during her career, and it is rumoured that one of the first dates Sean Penn ever took her on was a trip to Westwood Memorial Park, to pay her respects at Marilyn's grave.

This photo shows Madonna in her Marilyn style, at the 1991 Academy Awards.

Madonna

Madonna has worked with many photographers over the years, but one who became a particularly good friend was Herb Ritts. The two first met when he was commissioned to take publicity photos for *Desperately Seeking Susan*, and they went on to work together on many occasions, such as during the *True Blue* period, and on the first pop video he ever directed: "Cherish" from the *Like a Prayer* album.

The video was shot at the beach, and Madonna became so cold and wet that she swore she'd never work with Ritts again. Of course, she changed her mind the moment she saw the video and pictures from the shoot,

and the two remained very close. When Ritts passed away in 2002, Madonna was chosen to speak at his memorial. Choking back tears, the singer said that he was such a gentleman she couldn't even bribe him into saying a single swear word. She also described how he took some of the first photos of her daughter Lourdes, and continued to snap her children twice yearly for the next six years. She ended the speech by openly crying, and saying "I love you Herb".

This photo shows the two friends at the APLA Dance-a-thon benefit in April 1991.

Truth or Dare (aka *In Bed with Madonna*) is a 1991 documentary following Madonna's *Blond Ambition* tour and her time on the road. Directed by Alek Keshishian, the movie is a no-limits, behind-the-scenes look at the singers, dancers and crew, as well as the star herself.

The film was well-received at the box office, but was not without controversy; the singer was seen in a variety of revealing scenes, such as demonstrating oral sex on a bottle, taking the film crew to her mother's grave while her brother Christopher looks on without comment, talking about her teenage sexual antics with her best friend Moira, and revealing her brother Martin's personal problems. She was also seen pretending to stick her finger down her throat after Kevin Costner described the show as "neat", which apparently was to come back to haunt her later when he chose Whitney Houston over her as his leading lady in *The Bodyguard*.

This photo shows Madonna, brother Christopher and director Alek Keshishian at a screening for *Truth or Dare*.

In spite of certain corners of the media concentrating on negative parts of *Truth or Dare*, the documentary showed the sheer determination, strength and creativity required to create such a show as *Blond Ambition* and take it around the world. Because of this, *Truth or Dare* has become one of the most interesting and informative music documentaries ever made.

Madonna was incredibly proud of the finished product, and in order to publicise it, she took part in various interviews and appeared at several screenings. However, no appearance was as famous as the one she did when the film was screened at the Cannes Film Festival. Arriving wrapped in what appeared to be a pink silk sheet, Madonna posed for the cameras for a short time, before unwrapping herself to reveal a white pointy bra and underpants combo. The crowd, of course, went wild and the photographers couldn't get enough, as demonstrated in this picture.

During *Truth or Dare*, Madonna is seen flirting with a relatively unknown (at the time) actor called Antonio Banderas. In the film she freely admits having a crush on him and decides that when they meet, she will make him fall madly in love with her. However, even though the singer makes her desire more than obvious during their meeting, she hadn't reckoned on meeting his wife too. This effectively put paid to any plans she may have had to whisk him away, and the segment ends with Madonna complaining that she never heard from the actor again.

Several years later, Banderas was to become a much-admired film star and the husband of *Working Girl* actress Melanie Griffith. He also starred opposite Madonna in *Evita* in 1996, during which time the two had a very good working relationship.

This photo, taken five years before the making of *Evita*, is almost a foretelling of what was to come. Not only does it show the two actors together, but they are also at an event celebrating Andrew Lloyd Webber, one of the creators of *Evita*.

The early to mid-1990s saw Madonna taking small but significant parts in a variety of different movies, starting with the Woody Allen flick *Shadows and Fog*, released in March 1992. The film starred Allen himself, and co-starred Mia Farrow, Kathy Bates, Jodie Foster and John Malkovich, so Madonna was in good company when she took on the role of Marie, a tightrope artist in a circus. She later described it as a "blink and you'll miss me" part, though the experience of working with Allen was well worth it, and the part certainly gave her a whole new look.

At the beginning of filming, Madonna found the work to be quite confusing, thanks to the fact that Woody Allen wasn't the most sociable of directors and wouldn't say much to any of the actors on set. However, she later told interviewer Regis Philbin that he was still very much the boss: "He's a man in charge, which I have to admire. It was great." The director also gave everyone a great deal of flexibility in order to explore their characters. "That sort of freedom is sort of daunting," she told Philbin. "But he casts you perfectly and hires people to sort of exude what they already exude." Madonna went on to enjoy the experience and felt that Allen had really brought out the best in her as an actress and performer.

This photo shows Madonna in costume as Marie.

In July 1992, Madonna's next movie was released. Entitled *A League of Their Own*, it was inspired by the true story of the All-American Girls Professional Baseball League (AAGPBL). Out of all the movies Madonna had made up to this point, this one was probably the most successful in terms of reviews, and sported a host of famous actors, such as Tom Hanks, Geena Davis and Rosie O'Donnell.

While Davis and Hanks had the starring roles in the movie, Madonna's portrayal of "All the Way" Mae Mordabito was funny and heartfelt, while the chemistry she had with Rosie O'Donnell was clear for everyone to see. Director Penny Marshall teamed them up in the hope that they would be a good influence on each other, and the two ultimately went on to become great friends.

The movie – both hilarious and heart-breaking, but never boring – gave Madonna a chance to learn how to play baseball, and she earned more than her share of bruises throughout the production. But in spite of the physical activity, Marshall told Madonna to stop working out so much, as the muscles she brought with her to the set were not in keeping with the kind of body a young woman in the 1940s would probably have had. As well as acting in the movie, Madonna also provided the beautiful ballad "This Used to Be My Playground" for the soundtrack.

This photo shows Madonna on set with director Penny Marshall.

At the beginning of an era in Madonna's life that was to prove the most controversial, she took part in a fashion show for John Paul Gaultier, which was also attended by Billy Idol and Raquel Welch. Held in September 1992, the singer was seen walking down the catwalk with the designer himself, sporting what looked to be a plain, dark suit and matching beret. However, on reaching the end of the runway, after hesitating for a moment, she then took off her coat to reveal a blouse that can only be described as being a cross between an open bra and a pair of braces. Madonna wasn't wearing any undergarments, meaning that at this point her bare breasts were clearly on display.

Fans went wild and as she showed off a gold-toothed smile, several admirers tried to storm the stage but were held back by security. Finally, as the applause eventually died down, the singer hugged Jean Paul Gaultier and they made their way off stage.

This photo shows Madonna as she looked before revealing her assets to the audience.

While making *A League of Their Own*, Madonna had an idea for a book she wanted to write: a tome called *Sex*, which she worked on during the summer and released in late 1992. The book was full of pictures of the singer in all kinds of provocative positions – most of which were nude or semi-nude – and although popular with fans, it caused huge controversy in the media.

The book went on sale at midnight on 21 October, and legions of readers, reporters and those who were plain curious lined up in order to get a first glimpse of the much-anticipated book. However, the sealed metallic cover put paid to anyone who just wanted to peep inside, and made sure that if you wanted to see the book, it most certainly needed to be paid for. The ploy worked and *Sex* sold out very quickly.

Featured in the volume were the likes of actress Isabella Rossellini, model Naomi Campbell and love interests Tony Ward and Vanilla Ice, whom Madonna had enjoyed brief affairs with before the book's release. The text comprised of a league of sexual fantasies – some handwritten and others typed – and came across as more of a saucy scrapbook than a fully fledged erotic volume. Still, the critics were amazed that such a book was being published, and this particular project signified the start of a downturn in Madonna's career fortunes.

This photo shows Madonna at the book-launch party in New York.

At the same time as the publication of *Sex*, Madonna released an album entitled *Erotica*. It included hits such as "Rain" and "Bad Girl", as well as what looked to be a dig at Warren Beatty's romance with Annette Bening, "Thief of Hearts". However, the song that attracted the most attention was the title track, which was released with an S&M-inspired video showing Madonna acting as a dominatrix called Dita.

The promo for *Erotica* showed footage from the *Sex* book photo shoot, and was designed to look like a black-and-white home movie: grainy, with surface noise and uneven camera work. Of course MTV banned the video immediately, which prompted Madonna to release a statement declaring that her work was a "fantasy". In spite of that, she did say she understood the reason for banning it, as the channel was watched by a great deal of younger people that the song and video were not aimed at.

This photo shows Madonna in a publicity still for *Erotica*.

Around the time she was working on the *Sex* book, Madonna also landed the lead role in *Body of Evidence*, an erotic thriller which required her not only to disrobe, but also to perform in various revealing sex scenes. The film co-starred Willem Dafoe (playing a lawyer) and revolved around the story of Rebecca Carlson (Madonna) and the death of her lover, a wealthy man called Andrew Marsh. Rebecca is accused of killing him by inducing a heart attack brought on by sex, and the film is comprised of a mix of courtroom drama and passionate scenes between Rebecca and her lawyer.

The whole *Sex/Erotica/Body of Evidence* era was quickly labelled as Madonna's least popular. Her album sales plummeted and reviews for the film were dire, though in truth, many people still went to see it, even if just to complain about it afterwards. Madonna declared that this part of her career was a rebellion, "a statement on the hypocrisy of the world that we live in".

This photo shows Madonna as Rebecca Carlson in *Body of Evidence*.

As part of the promotion for *Erotica*, Madonna chatted to British interviewer Jonathan Ross at London's Hyde Park Hotel. After fighting his way through throngs of fans, he met the star, who was dressed in a suit, tie and beret. They then discussed the projects she was involved with, as well as her love of wearing a gold tooth and her aborted attempts to write a song with Michael Jackson. However, one of the most interesting parts of the interview came when the two talked about Maverick, the company Madonna had recently set up in order to make records, books and films.

Maverick ensured that the singer was twice as busy as she had ever been before, and while she assured Ross that finding "another Madonna" was not possible, she did say that she was committed to discovering someone cutting edge and relevant. This search involved Madonna signing and mentoring various different acts, including Alanis Morissette and the Prodigy, as well as releasing her own albums on the label too. Madonna was associated with Maverick until the mid-2000s, when she sold her shares to Warner Brothers, and in recent years the label has been extremely quiet.

This photo shows Madonna and Ross in a publicity shot for the interview.

Dangerous Game (aka *Snake Eyes*) was a 1993 movie starring Madonna as Sarah Jennings and Harvey Keitel as Eddie Israel. The movie was a complicated one thanks to the fact that it was something of a movie-within-a-movie, concentrating on Israel's attempts to make a film starring Jennings and Francis Burns (played by James Russo).

The film was shot in a grainy, almost voyeuristic way, and much of it was said to have been improvised. The result was a confusing storyline which turned many fans and critics off, and Madonna disliked it so much that she refused to be involved with the publicity surrounding its release. Director Abel Ferrara later slammed the singer for criticising the movie, telling *A.V. Club* interviewer Scott Tobias that he had never experienced an actor bad-mouth a film and would never forgive her for it.

This photo shows Madonna during the making of the movie, wearing glasses and a rare (for this film) smile.

In spite of Madonna's distaste for *Dangerous Game*, the movie remains interesting for one scene – where Sarah Jennings explains to Eddie Israel that she was once raped on the roof of a building. This seemingly improvised scene is noteworthy because of the fact that Madonna herself was raped, shortly after moving to New York at the beginning of her career.

The incident has been reported on at various points during the singer's career, and Madonna herself referred to it briefly in an article she wrote in 2013 for *Harper's Bazaar*. In the piece, she explained that an unknown attacker dragged her up to the top of a building with a knife in her back. She went no deeper into the story, but the scene in *Dangerous Game* seems to give a more detailed and thorough look at what most likely happened during this terrible period in Madonna's early career.

This photo shows the dishevelled actress, sitting on the floor with Harvey Keitel, during *Dangerous Game*.

Madonna's next tour – *The Girlie Show* – was very much inspired by the idea of circus and carnival, when it toured the world from September to December 1993. During this time the singer had her hair cut extremely short, and many of the dancers were asked to shave their heads in order to achieve something of an androgynous look.

The tour kicked off at Wembley Stadium, London, but while the crowd seemed to absolutely love the spectacle on stage, the media were not impressed. Some claimed it to be the worst tour in Madonna's history, and while it is true that it wasn't on the same level as *Blond Ambition*, that description is rather unfair.

The first half of the show included songs such as "Erotica", "Vogue", "Express Yourself" and "Deeper and Deeper", and some beautiful choreography during "Rain". Gene Kelly himself had advised Madonna on the choreography for the number, and while some of what he put together was not used, his inspiration was still apparent.

This photo and the one on the next page show Madonna at Wembley Stadium, during the London leg of the tour.

The second half of the show contained a tribute to Marlene Dietrich, in the form of "Like a Virgin" and "Bye Bye Baby", before going on to a madcap rendition of "I'm Going Bananas". "Holiday" was done as a patriotic song, complete with American flag and marching interlude. However, by the time the show reached the final stages, including "Justify My Love", it was all change again, and suddenly a top-hatted Madonna appeared with elaborately dressed dancers. The last song was "Everybody", which had never been used as a finale song before, and perhaps didn't have the same effect as more upbeat songs, but even so, Madonna got it to work.

Throughout the evening, a clown was seen dancing on the stage, and although this was played by a dancer for most of the concert, by the end it was Madonna herself in the costume. Alone on stage, she revealed herself to the crowd, before finally bringing the curtain down on the show.

Madonna has been friends with nightclub owner Ingrid Casares ever since she met her through Sandra Bernard in the early 1990s. However, perhaps the period when they were most seen together was in the mid-1990s, when Madonna spent a lot of time in Miami, where Ingrid lived and worked.

It was during this period of time that Madonna seemed be going through a transitional stage between the *Sex* book and her *Evita* era. She appeared on David Letterman's show and swore so many times that it was feared the programme would be taken off air, then she was seen with the bad boy of basketball, Dennis Rodman. He would later write some less-than-perfect remarks about her in his autobiography, and go on to claim that Madonna wanted to marry him and have his child. However, the star told Oprah Winfrey that they only dated for two months, that she did not want his child and that what he wrote in the book was fiction.

This photo shows Madonna and Ingrid Casares at a Florida hotel in 1994, around the time of the Rodman/Letterman brouhaha.

In April 1994, a film entitled *With Honors*, directed by Madonna's friend and business partner Alek Keshishian, was released. The movie was a comedy/drama about a student, Monty (played by Brendan Fraser), and Simon, a homeless man (played by Joe Pesci), who eventually become friends after the latter is accused of stealing a university thesis. The movie was released to fairly negative reviews, and is rarely played on television today, but it did give the world a brand new Madonna song after the singer was asked by Keshishian to write the soundtrack.

The ballad, entitled "I'll Remember", was a beautiful accompaniment to the film, and the video showed clips from the movie, as well as of Madonna looking quite similar to the way she had looked in the "Rain" video, with extremely short, dark hair and a long dress, standing in front of a microphone. The song reached number one in several countries, but stopped at number seven in the official UK chart.

This photo shows Madonna and Alek at the Los Angeles premiere of *With Honors*.

When Madonna appeared in the 1992 Gaultier fashion show, she caused scandal in the media after revealing her bare breasts on stage. However, when she returned in October 1994, it was all change. This time the venue was complete with old fairground carousels and other paraphernalia, and as Madonna made her way on the catwalk, she was seen wearing a beautiful gold dress, curled hair piled on top of her head, and an elaborate headpiece.

The singer was pushing an old-fashioned baby's pram, inside of which was not a child but a small puppy looking very much like a Bichon Frise. By the time she reached the end of the runway, Madonna had picked the dog up and kissed it, before finally walking back off stage, clothes still fully intact.

This photo shows Madonna at the show, pushing the pram along the catwalk.

Madonna's next album was *Bedtime Stories*, released in October 1994. Coming off the back of the *Sex* book era, the album didn't do as well as earlier releases and failed to reach number one in many of the countries it was available in. The anger at the way she had been treated in the past few years was evident in the song "Human Nature", which had an accompanying video showing the singer trussed up in bondage gear. Other videos included "Take a Bow", featuring a failed romance with a bullfighter, and "Secret", a black-and-white film in which Madonna sang while walking through Harlem.

Perhaps the most ambitious of all the songs was "Bedtime Story", written by Björk. It had a futuristic, euphoric feel, with a video to match, and was showcased during the 1995 Brit Awards, as can be seen from this photograph. During the performance, Madonna wore long, blonde hair extensions and a dress that was blown around steadily by a wind machine, while dancers performed a variety of moves behind her.

The launch of *Bedtime Stories* took Madonna around the world in order to publicise it. One interview was given to US-turned-UK interviewer Ruby Wax, who chatted with the star in Paris. Later, Wax would criticise her own handling of the interview, saying she was intimidated by Madonna's entourage and that nerves got the better of her. This forced her to ask questions that – in her own words – made no sense, or seemed to show anger. It is clear that Wax sees the entire experience as an absolute failure, and has talked about it frequently, incorporating it into seminars to demonstrate things that can go wrong while interacting with clients and co-workers.

Actually, however, while Wax may see it as a catastrophe, most fans think of it as one of Madonna's best ever interviews. The problems that Wax describes are not apparent on screen, and while it is true that things seemed a little tense at first, by the end the two looked like gal-pals, gossiping about men, sex, pets, children, hair and all the things that most interviewers don't ever talk to Madonna about. It may have been painful for Wax during filming, but in terms of showing another side to the star, the interview was a magnificent triumph.

This photo shows Madonna at a Paris fashion show, taken during the *Bedtime Stories* publicity tour, around the time of the Wax interview.

Madonna met fitness instructor Carlos Leon whilst jogging in New York's Central Park in 1994, and the two hit it off immediately. They began dating, and in 1996 welcomed their daughter, Lourdes Maria Ciccone Leon, into the world. By 1997 the two had parted ways, though, with some people falsely claiming that Madonna used him only as a sperm donor, and had no intention of ever letting him see the child.

These rumours were extremely unfair. Not only has Carlos contributed to the upbringing of his child since she was born, but he also describes her as the love of his life. He has remained close to Madonna too and over the years has been photographed regularly at her concerts and other events. When his daughter was young, Carlos was often seen at the park, not only enjoying time with her, but with Madonna's son Rocco too.

This photo shows the couple embracing at a party, towards the beginning of their relationship, before Madonna became pregnant with Lourdes.

In March 1995, to celebrate the
video for the single "Bedtime Story",
Madonna decided to treat her fans to
a pyjama party at New York's Webster
Hall. She arrived wearing a leopard-
print coat, with her hair in curls,
before revealing a silk nightdress
underneath her outerwear, much to
the delight of waiting photographers.
Inside the venue, a screening of the
"Bedtime Story" video was shown and
a DJ played music, helped by Madonna
herself during the early part of the
evening.

Later, as she sat on a large bed,
the singer read from a copy of the
children's book *Miss Spider's Tea
Party*, and shushed fans who were
interrupting the reading with screams
and shouts. Finally, after changing her
nightwear several times during the
course of the evening, it was time for
a quick dance before heading home to
bed for real.

This photo shows Madonna after
the book reading, dancing and quite
literally hanging out with her pyjama-
wearing fans and admirers.

Madonna has been a big fan of Muhammad Ali for many years, and when she eventually met him, he presented her with a signed photo, declaring both of them to be "the greatest". In June 1995 it was Madonna's turn to hold a presentation for Ali, when she appeared at a Parkinson's Disease Foundation benefit at the Marriot Marquis Hotel in New York. Wearing a conservative suit, the singer told the audience about the photo he had given her, and the thoughts he had written about them being the greatest. "I had to agree," she laughingly told the audience. The singer also explained that she had more photos of the boxer on her wall than anyone, including her family.

As Ali took to the stage, Madonna told the audience that she believed him to be the best boxer in the world. She then presented an award to her hero, and they went backstage in order to pose together for photographs, one of which can be seen opposite.

In June 1995, Madonna took a small cameo role in Spike Lee's movie *Girl 6*. The film told the story of Judy (played by Theresa Randle), an aspiring actress who is feeling disheartened by the entire industry. She tries many jobs, but in the end decides to work as a phone-sex operator, and it is during this part of the film that she meets Boss #3, played by Madonna. Boss #3 tells Judy about the kinds of things she will need to talk to clients about, which includes a large and varied range of kinky subjects, until finally she mentions that the job will take place at home. Having a shared telephone, Judy decides that working from home is not for her, and does not take the job.

Apart from one other small part, that is really the extent of Madonna's role in the movie. It opened to decidedly mixed reviews, though by the time it was released, Madonna was heavily into making *Evita* and probably didn't mind too much, if she even noticed at all.

This photo shows Madonna in the role of Boss #3, along with Spike Lee and Theresa Randle.

Madonna has appeared in various well-known ad campaigns over the years, such as the infamous Pepsi commercial, and later the ones for her own clothing line. However, she has also been in many more that are less known, including several for the Japanese market. Some of the first came for Mitsubishi, during 1986, when the singer is seen looking very much as she does in parts of the "Papa Don't Preach" video, wandering around a room full of books and videos to the tune of "True Blue". Another included the same kind of theme, but this time she appeared dressed in a bolero outfit, dancing along to "La Isla Bonita".

Several others followed, including one where Madonna is seen in a straight, blonde wig, declaring that everything is "just perfect". In 1991 she paid tribute to Marilyn Monroe's Madison Square Garden appearance on an elephant, and then almost twenty years later, she appeared in an advert for apartment buildings.

This screen-grab shows the singer in a 1995 advert for Takara where she is seen slaying a dragon before holding a much-earned drink.

After the MTV Video Music Awards in September 1995, Madonna had just sat down for a chat with interviewer Kurt Loder when wild rocker Courtney Love began heading in their direction. As Madonna was talking, suddenly a make-up compact was hurled straight over her head, and as she turned round to see what was going on, Loder can be heard on the footage of the interview asking if they should invite the Hole singer on stage with them. "Oh don't, please," Madonna replied but it was too late; Courtney was already running up the stairs to greet the pair and make her presence known.

Once she sat down, Courtney immediately began talking about how Madonna had said something mean about her in the past. Ever the height of calm and control, Madonna very politely told her that she hadn't been mean to anyone, and looked cautiously over to her entourage. It was clear very early on that Courtney didn't seem to be entirely sober, so as soon as they could, Madonna's people literally grabbed the singer's hand and took her down the stairs. Courtney then took over the interview, before finally falling off her stool, flat onto her back with legs sticking straight up in the air.

This photo shows Madonna at the awards show, before her evening was hijacked by Courtney Love.

Madonna had a small but entertaining role in the movie *Blue in the Face*, about the characters that frequent a Brooklyn cigar store. Released in October 1995, the much-improved movie featured appearances by Roseanne Barr, Michael J. Fox, Lily Tomlin and Lou Reed, and was billed as a follow-up to the Harvey Keitel movie *Smoke*.

During her small scene, Madonna appeared on a Brooklyn street, dressed as a singing telegram. Wearing a bright red and orange dress, with matching hat, she asks Harvey Keitel if he has seen Mr Augustus Wren.

When he assures her that he is the man she's looking for, Madonna's character hands over a telegram and launches into a funny – if not slightly embarrassing – song, telling him that a deal he has been concerned about is now off. At the end of the song, he thanks her and hands over a $5 tip. She then walks off camera, leaving Keitel to celebrate the news.

The film was never going to win Madonna any acting awards, but it did give her the chance to work once again with Harvey Keitel, and added another string to her acting bow.

Christopher Ciccone was always thought to be the closest of all Madonna's siblings to the singer. He was frequently seen as a dancer at the beginning of her career, as well as being interior designer for some of her homes and set designer on two tours. However, while on the outside the pair seemed like best friends, underneath the relationship can be best described as complicated and at times rather rocky.

This photograph shows the brother and sister in late 1995, looking happy and relaxed in each other's company. However, in 2008, Christopher released a tell-all book about his famous sister, after the two had fallen out a little time before. Madonna has remained tight-lipped about her thoughts on the subject, though it would be a fair presumption to say she was not pleased. Since then the relationship has remained – publicly at least – somewhat distant, though it has been said that the pair have exchanged some friendly emails in recent years.

After being the brunt of many jokes for some time, mainly thanks to the *Sex/ Erotica/Body of Evidence* era, Madonna decided to change her image again, this time to a stripped-back look reminiscent of some of the styles she tried during 1986. To add to this change, in November 1995 the singer decided to release an album entitled *Something to Remember*, a compilation of ballads from the past years, as well as two new songs, "You'll See" and "One More Chance", and a cover of the Marvin Gaye song "I Want You".

In the album notes, Madonna explained that the reason behind releasing an album of ballads lay in the fact that, as there had been so much controversy in her career, little attention had been paid to her music. She added that it was her wish to rectify this by releasing a simple album of songs "from my heart".

Her new image worked wonders, and with the making of *Evita* just around the corner, this was to become one of the most worthwhile and talked-about periods of her career.

In late 1995, Madonna was summoned to England, where she was to begin recording the soundtrack for the forthcoming movie *Evita*, with Antonio Banderas and Jimmy Nail. Madonna never made any secret of the fact that she disliked England in the early days, thanks to the media intrusion she always encountered. With that in mind, it can be assumed that spending time there during the recording of the soundtrack was not something she was particularly looking forward to. When recording began, the cast – along with director Alan Parker – had a great deal of work to make sure everything was done right. Madonna worked with a singing coach, and Parker later admitted that musically, everyone was in uncharted territory.

"It was hard to know if we hadn't all gone mad," he said in an interview.

However, after spending a little more time in the studio, the company built up a good working relationship, and the singer not only seemed to settle into the work, but also her surroundings. She kept a particularly low profile during the trip, but in her spare time enjoyed shopping, alone and incognito. She can be seen here quietly browsing the videos in a shop on Sloane Street in London.

Eventually, after spending several months recording songs such as "Don't Cry for Me Argentina" and the new track "You Must Love Me", Madonna left London, but it would not be long before she returned to shoot part of the movie in April 1996.

A small but entertaining movie role came in the form of *Four Rooms*, which was released in December 1995. The film revolved around four stories – each by a different director – with one thing in common: Ted the bellboy, and his adventures at the hotel during one memorable New Year's Eve.

In Madonna's section of the film, she played a witch staying in the Honeymoon Suite with her other coven members, all looking for a missing ingredient in order to reverse a spell cast on their goddess (played by Amanda De Cadenet). Poor Ted has just what they need to complete the spell (his semen) and after some reluctance, he agrees to provide it. Madonna was drawn to the role because, while the women were meant to be seen as somewhat freakish, the way they all interacted with each other was completely natural. She liked that particular side of it and while it certainly can't be said that the film gained many plaudits, she did have fun in the role.

This photo shows Madonna in the lobby of the hotel, having just met the shy but accommodating Ted.

If ever there was a mammoth fight to win a part in a movie, it was the one Madonna undertook to get the role of Eva Peron in *Evita*. From the late 1980s, the singer had been talking about the role, declaring that she was the only one who could play Peron, and trying desperately to fight off other contenders, such as Meryl Streep and Michelle Pfeiffer. In the end she decided to write an impassioned plea to director Alan Parker, which certainly gained his attention, and after several meetings the role was hers. After recording the soundtrack in late 1995, and then celebrating Christmas at home in the States, Madonna and the other cast members – including Antonio Banderas and Jonathan Pryce – travelled to Argentina in order to start filming.

Despite Madonna being passionately committed to the part, she faced demonstrations and abuse on her arrival in Buenos Aires, as some people felt that having a pop singer as the late President's wife would somehow tarnish her saintly image. Madonna carried on regardless and travelled round the city, visiting Eva Peron's friends and interviewing them about what she was like in real life. All of the research she did went into her creation of Eva, and the actress spent hours studying photographs, watching documentaries and reading books in order to perfect her part.

This photograph shows Madonna ascending a flight of stairs, dressed as Eva Peron.

The *Evita* shoot was not the easiest of experiences, particularly for Madonna, who discovered she was pregnant just after the crew left Argentina and headed to Europe for the next stage of shooting. Although the singer wanted to keep news of her pregnancy a secret, for the sake of the production she had to tell several people on set, particularly the dress designers, who spent many hours adjusting her costumes to make way for her growing bump. But sometimes it proved hard to hide the pregnancy completely, and this is apparent in several scenes in the movie where furs, bags and other items were used to try to cover the singer's stomach.

Costumes weren't the only thing to cause problems during production, and there were several points when Madonna feared that the dancing involved would harm the baby. Doctors were called to the Pinewood Studios set on at least one occasion after she felt unwell, and after being examined, the singer was relieved to discover that everything was fine.

In the end, the film was completed without serious incident, and Madonna soon declared it to be the greatest professional accomplishment of her life.

This photo shows Madonna and Jonathan Pryce filming a scene in front of a blue screen at Pinewood Studios, England.

While Madonna was heavily involved in both *Evita* and her pregnancy, she was approached by John F. Kennedy Junior to pose as his mother, Jackie, in an upcoming issue of *George* magazine. The idea excited the young publisher, but not so much Madonna, who wrote back addressing him as "Johnny Boy" and joking that she couldn't possibly portray his mother as her eyebrows weren't thick enough.

The letter could be considered a little too informal if not for the fact that the two knew each other quite well and were rumoured to be involved in a short-lived affair, either while the singer was separated from Sean Penn or shortly after their divorce. While it had been a very low-key relationship, meeting for the most part in a gym they both frequented, they were seen several times together, as this hazy photo, taken around 1988/89 shows. Madonna was said to be smitten by the handsome bachelor, but his mother was not so thrilled with the blonde, and the relationship eventually fizzled out, though the two remained cordial until Kennedy's death in a plane crash in 1999.

Several months after completing *Evita*, and after what seemed to be a very guarded pregnancy, Lourdes Marie Ciccone Leon (known as Lola) was born on 14 October 1996. The world's press gathered outside the hospital for a glimpse of the newborn, but they were out of luck. Both mother and baby were escorted quietly out of the building and quickly taken to Madonna's mansion before anyone could take a photo of the most famous new parent in the world.

Madonna hoped for a few months of peace and privacy in order to get to know her daughter and recover from her emergency C-section delivery, but an enterprising journalist put paid to that. "Borrowing" a corner of her neighbour's window (the only one that overlooked her property), the man happily snapped photos of Madonna and baby in their garden, showing the singer dressed in a white nightgown and with unstyled hair. Photos were also taken of her receiving gifts from local children whilst standing on her front doorstep. When they were published she was understandably furious, and the venture ultimately backfired for the media because from then on the singer went out of her way to keep Lourdes out of the public eye as much as she possibly could.

This photo shows Madonna carrying her baby in December 1996.

Evita was premiered in Los Angeles, several months after the birth of Lourdes. During her first official appearance after giving birth, Madonna walked the red carpet with boyfriend Carlos Leon, dressed in an extraordinary Eva Peron-inspired gown and hat.

This was to be the first of many appearances around the world, and for each one the singer dressed for the part in elegant suits, dresses and hats. Her hair, meanwhile, was either pulled back dramatically from her face or worn down over her shoulders in a sleek, layered style. Lourdes travelled with her famous mother, and of course many of the interviewers were interested in how the young child was getting along. Madonna, it should be said, was always happy to oblige their queries, and juggled the job of mother and superstar by taking regular breaks from the press junkets in order to go upstairs to her hotel room and feed the young baby.

This photo shows an *Evita*-inspired Madonna, waving from a balcony during the Italian leg of her publicity tour.

Madonna's performance in *Evita* wowed the crowds and critics alike, and she became the hot favourite to win at both the Golden Globes and Academy Awards during 1997. First came the Golden Globes, where she won the very well-deserved award for best actress. Her speech, during which she declared herself "incredibly blessed", was heartfelt and humble, and rumours circulated that an Oscar would most definitely be in her future. Unfortunately, while *Evita* itself was nominated in several categories, Madonna failed to pick up any nominations for her performance, which many people still believe was an absolute travesty.

Despite not being nominated for her role, Madonna rose above it all, and actually went to the Academy Awards ceremony in order to sing a beautiful rendition of "You Must Love Me", from the official soundtrack. The song won an Oscar for Andrew Lloyd Webber and Tim Rice, and Madonna was absolutely delighted.

This photo shows Madonna and Carlos Leon walking the red carpet at the Golden Globes.

While much has been said about Madonna's admiration of old Hollywood stars such as Marilyn Monroe and Marlene Dietrich, probably the actress she admires beyond all others is Elizabeth Taylor. In February 1997, during a televised special, the singer took to the stage in order to give a speech about the actress and to tell the world just how much she admired her, both as a child and an adult. During the presentation, she described how Taylor seemed to have a luminous light that took her breath away, and that she deeply regretted that the actress had retired from the screen.

Madonna then went on to talk about the courage and strength Elizabeth showed in inspiring and sharing her thoughts on AIDS and what needed to be done to raise awareness and prevent infection. "You are the most golden of stars," she told Taylor, before helping her on to the stage. The audience broke into spontaneous applause and gave the actress a standing ovation.

This photo shows Madonna and Elizabeth Taylor posing together after her speech.

While pregnant with daughter Lourdes, Madonna was introduced to a yoga teacher who specialised in a pre-natal version of the ancient practice. The singer toyed with the idea of taking it up, and by the time her daughter was born, she was ready to take it seriously, trying several different branches until one – Ashtanga – caught her interest.

Ashtanga is a very physical practice which heats the body through flowing from one posture to another. It is tough and extremely hard to master if the student is not particularly fit, but it was no surprise that Madonna took to it straight away, shelving most other methods of exercise as soon as she began her classes. She later told Oprah Winfrey that she was now "gym free", and also expressed to her official fan club that she summoned creativity through "yoga, yoga, yoga".

Her practice was something Madonna took seriously for a long time, immersing herself in the theory as well as the physical side. Unfortunately, a horse accident in 2006 made it difficult to do much yoga at all, and she eventually found her way back to the gym.

When yoga came into Madonna's life, another passion wasn't far behind, as she began looking at her existence in a very different way. She began to address questions she had been avoiding for years, such as why was she here? What was her purpose? What was she meant to be doing with her life? She spoke about this to a friend, who suggested that the singer look into Kabbalah, an ancient wisdom that is said to provide tools to enjoy a better way of living. Madonna did look into it and began undertaking classes at the Kabbalah centre in Los Angeles. Once there, she was taught to take responsibility for any chaos she had in her life, and encouraged to accept that she was solely in charge of her own destiny.

Madonna has been studying Kabbalah ever since her first introduction, and is frequently seen wearing a red string around her wrist, a talisman said to ward off negative thoughts and misfortune. Both yoga and the discovery of Kabbalah changed Madonna's outlook forever, and while it frequently irritates her critics, the singer continues to be inspired and guided by it to the present day. Her family are also frequently photographed going in and out of Kabbalah centres around the world, wearing red strings on their wrists.

This photo shows the change of image Madonna undertook when she first began her studies into Kabbalah: the long hair, flowing skirt and happier disposition.

When Diana, Princess of Wales was killed in a Paris car crash in August 1997, the world was in shock. Madonna was not immune to the sadness and spoke about how she had been chased by paparazzi through the very same tunnel on various occasions during her life. The star had met the princess just once, and ironically the two spoke for several minutes about the media and the constant pursuit by photographers. They had promised to meet up on a more informal basis shortly afterwards, but it was not to be; instead Madonna found herself speaking several times about the tragedy, in print, interviews and speeches.

One such time was during the VMA awards, shortly after Princess Diana's death. During her speech, Madonna told the audience that it was time for everyone – including herself – to take responsibility for the insatiable need to pursue gossip, rumours and stories. She also spoke about the princess during a 1998 interview with Oprah, where she described that summer as being devastating. "Didn't you feel haunted?" she asked Oprah. "Didn't you feel like you had to hold on to the walls?" Madonna also described that after the death of the princess, she felt as though it was a giant wake-up call. "It was a big slap in the face to humanity," she said.

This photograph shows Madonna at the VMA Awards in 1997, during which she gave her speech about Diana.

Ray of Light was Madonna's next studio album, released in February 1998. The album was the first written after the birth of her daughter, and Madonna quickly declared it to be the greatest music she had ever created as well as the most fun she'd ever had in a studio. This was also the view of her fan base, who rushed out and bought not only the album, but the various singles released from it, such as the title track "Ray of Light", "Frozen", "The Power of Goodbye" and "Drowned World/Substitute for Love". The album was co-produced by William Orbit and greatly influenced by her study of yoga and Kabbalah. As a result, Madonna's softer side was there for all to see, especially in the beautiful track entitled "Little Star", written especially for her little girl.

The singer promoted the album sporting long, curly hair, Indian-inspired clothes and henna tattoos, and appeared to be finally at peace with herself and her life. She told reporters, "I feel like I've been on a very intense journey; I feel like I've had a lot of revelations and I feel like I look at the world differently now." However, she may have been a softer diva, but if journalists thought she was a pushover they were very much mistaken. As her fortieth birthday approached, she was cheekily asked if she was scared of getting older. "No," she snapped, before adding a cutting, "are you?"

While Madonna was still frequently followed around by paparazzi, all trying to catch a glimpse of her daughter, the singer continued to try to keep her life under wraps as much as she possibly could. However, in March 1998 the first official photos were released to *Vanity Fair*, showing Madonna dressed simply and naturally, balancing the curly-haired tot on her lap and lying down on her stomach.

Taken by photographer and friend Mario Testino, the pictures were presented, Madonna said, because she felt that giving official photos to the press would prevent them from trying to snap unofficial shots whilst the two were out and about. It worked for a time and they were offered a little more privacy, but as this photo shows, they weren't totally immune to being followed. Since then, Lourdes, along with Madonna's other children, have been frequently photographed going about their daily lives, though at this stage at least, they all seem to take it – for the most part – in their stride.

While this photo of Madonna and Elton John at a rainforest benefit in April 1998 seems to show the two getting along famously together, this has not always been the case. Elton has been vocal about his distaste for the singer on various occasions, including criticising her lip synching in concert, and apparently declaring that her attempt at a Bond song in 2002 was the worst he had ever heard.

Things came to a head in 2012 during the Golden Globe Awards, when the two were up against each other in the best song category. On the red carpet, Elton told an interviewer that his songwriting rival didn't have a chance of winning; only he didn't put it in such an eloquent way. When Madonna was told about the remarks, she jokingly called it "fighting words"

and added "may the best man win". Later that evening, Madonna did indeed win the award, and whilst giving her acceptance speech, the camera cut away to reveal Elton's reaction; the look on his face said it all.

Elton's husband, David Furnish, also got in on the act by making several less-than-praising comments about the singer, but when Madonna was asked about the spat backstage, she told reporters, "I hope he speaks to me for the next couple of years. He's known to get mad at me." Some months later, however, Elton saw Madonna in a restaurant, and sent over a note apologising for what he had said about her. The singer accepted his apology and he paid for her dinner; thus ending one of the biggest showbiz feuds in history ... for now.

Madonna is a keen advocate for safe sex, and the importance of educating people on what AIDS is – and what it is not. She was one of the first celebrities to lend her time to AIDS charities and awareness; possibly because several of her loved ones – including her dance teacher Christopher Flynn and friend Martin Burgoyne – have lived with (and later succumbed to) HIV/AIDS.

Over the years, Madonna has lent her time to many fundraising and awareness causes, such as an advert in 1988 which told youngsters how to protect themselves against HIV. A year later she took part in an AIDS Dance-a-Thon, which saw her tearing up the dance floor for an hour and giving a speech about issues close to her heart. Next to her was Christopher Flynn, who explained that the singer was the first person he turned to when he was diagnosed with HIV.

This photo shows an event in September 1998, when the singer contributed to AIDS Walk Los Angeles and gave a passionate speech about funding programmes to educate youngsters about the disease. During the event she also criticised the government for not spending their money on the likes of needle exchange programmes.

In 1998, Johnny Vaughan was one of the hottest interviewers around, and it was no surprise when Madonna chose him as the host for her only UK interview, towards the end of the year. Sporting straight, glossy hair and a burgundy leather jacket, the interview was different from others she had given thanks to the fact that Johnny is very unaffected by celebrity and Madonna seemed to get along well with him because of this. At one point she even stared at him intently and addressed the fact that he seemed to have broken his nose.

She also became very interested in his star sign and explained the workings of astrology to him as the interview progressed.

The chat ended up being one of the most memorable and casual of all the ones she had done, though it was later revealed that the two did not get off to a good start when Madonna presented Vaughan with a necklace that did not fit properly around his neck. She apparently barked at him to take it off and in some scenes of the interview he can be seen clutching the offending item in his left hand.

All of the hard work Madonna put into the *Ray of Light* album finally paid off when, in February 1999, she received four Grammy Awards, much to her delight. Arriving at the venue for the ceremony, Madonna told reporters that she was shaking and nervous; an uncharacteristic trait, which she put down to the fact that she was opening the show on what was a very important evening.

After performing "Nothing Really Matters", complete with Geisha attire, Madonna then picked up awards for Best Pop Album, Best Dance Recording, Best Music Video and then an additional award for the design of *Ray of Light*. While accepting the award for Best Pop Album, she thanked all those who worked on it. "I share this Grammy with each and every one of you," she declared. Afterwards Madonna celebrated the evening with a vodka cocktail and told reporters, "I am very happy and blessed."

This photo shows the singer posing with her four awards.

In early 1999, Madonna became the face of the Max Factor cosmetics company and took part in several television and print commercials. The photographs from the campaign show Madonna in full colour, with auburn hair and more than a hint of the old-time glamour of Jean Harlow, Bette Davis and others.

The television adverts went for a slightly more informal style, shot in a sepia tone and showing the actress in front of the mirror, laughing and joking alongside her make-up artist Sarah Monzani. As well as showing Madonna's sense of humour, the commercial also demonstrated just how much time the star had been spending in England, as her new accent was there for all to hear.

Madonna loved the look so much that she kept it for her attendance at the 1999 Academy Awards. This photograph shows Madonna at the *Vanity Fair* party afterwards, sitting with close friend Ingrid Casares.

One of the biggest loves of Madonna's life entered her world in 1999. Movie director Guy Ritchie was invited to a lunch at the home of Sting and his wife Trudie Styler, and Madonna arrived with her then-boyfriend Andy Bird. Some years later, the singer told interviewers Regis Philbin and Kelly Ripa that the two were not speaking to each other at the time, so Bird sat at one side of the table while Madonna found herself seated next to Guy Ritchie at the other. The couple got along very well; she enjoyed his company and he jokingly told her that he might be able to get her a part in one of his movies. Madonna loved his sense of humour and ended up inviting him over to her house for tea, which he did, arriving a day earlier than planned.

After that encounter, Madonna's relationship with Andy Bird eventually ended and she began a very quiet – but rumoured – relationship with Ritchie. Together they went out on dates together, but all the time made a point of not being photographed. Madonna was also spotted on the set of Ritchie's movie *Snatch*, though when asked about it, both laughed off the accusation that they were anything but just good friends.

Finally they made their first official appearance in February 2000, at the Savoy hotel, during the *Evening Standard* Film Awards. This photo shows the pair happily posing for photographers during the course of the evening.

In spring 1999, Madonna embarked on a new film project, *The Next Best Thing*. The movie saw her in the role of Abbie Reynolds, opposite Rupert Everett who played her gay best friend, Robert. The plot revolved around the idea that after a drunken night together, the two friends end up having a child, though their idea of living as a thoroughly modern family quickly turns sour when Abbie falls for Ben, played by Benjamin Bratt.

The idea for the movie originally came to Madonna through friend Rupert Everett, after the two had wanted to work together for a long time. He developed the project for them both and Madonna signed on for it because it gave her the opportunity to work not only with Everett, but with director John Schlesinger too. It is interesting to note that, while Madonna plays a yoga teacher in the final movie, when she was first cast as Abbie, the character was originally a swimming instructor. Madonna changed it because of her love of yoga at the time.

This photo shows Madonna, Everett and director John Schlesinger during the filming of *The Next Best Thing*.

In May 1999, Madonna released "Beautiful Stranger", the theme tune for the Mike Myers movie *Austin Powers: The Spy Who Shagged Me*. It was accompanied by a psychedelic video, starring Madonna as a "master of disguise" and Myers as – of course – Austin Powers. It was a colourful, fun-filled video and showed the singer not only cavorting playfully with Myers, but also singing on stage to a room full of eager dancers.

There is a story that the song was written for Madonna's one-time boyfriend Andy Bird, whom she dated during the *Ray of Light* period. It is said that when the two split up, she penned the song and left a message on his answer machine, telling him all about it. It is not known if he ever replied, but Bird did make the headlines shortly afterwards when he apparently got into a scuffle with Madonna's new boyfriend, director Guy Ritchie.

This photo shows Madonna at the premiere of the movie *Ideal Husband*, which was released around the same time as "Beautiful Stranger", and shows her sporting the same kind of look as the one worn in the video.

While Madonna is more often associated with designer Stella McCartney, it was her dad, ex-Beatle Paul, whom she was spotted with during the 1999 MTV awards, held in September of that year. After receiving an award for her single "Beautiful Stranger", the singer was then honoured by a series of drag-artist lookalikes, who took the audience through various aspects of Madonna's career from the beginning to the present day. Finally she took to the stage herself, in order to thank the artists and describe the whole experience as "freaky".

After all this, Madonna gave a glowing introduction to Paul McCartney, describing how nervous she was when preparing the speech, and declaring him an inspiration and a cool dad. When McCartney took to the stage, calling her "babe", it was clear that the two felt perfectly at ease in each other's company; so much so in fact that the press wondered if there was something romantic going on between them. This rumour actually amused Madonna, who later dismissed the story, saying that it was perfectly clear to everyone that she preferred to date younger men.

By autumn 1999, Madonna's attentions turned to making a new album, which was to be the first since the critically acclaimed *Ray of Light*. Once again William Orbit was asked to be part of some of the songs, but this time she decided to also enlist the help of French producer Mirwais Ahmadzai. Unfortunately, because of the language barrier between Mirwais and Madonna, the first few days in the studio were tough, and the singer did not know if she would be able to get anything on tape at all. Thankfully they overcame the obstacles and the album was recorded in late 1999 through to early 2000.

This photo shows Madonna at the beginning of recording, when she took time out to visit a Versace show in New York. While she did not wish to give anything away about the nature of the upcoming album, she did reveal one thing in her decision to wear a cowboy hat – albeit a leopard-print one – which would be a prominent theme in the artwork and videos for the new record.

The Next Best Thing needed a soundtrack, and co-star Rupert Everett believed that "American Pie" by Don McLean would be a wonderful choice. Furthermore, he planned that, while Madonna could sing the track, he would do backing vocals. Madonna wasn't so keen and insisted that she would only perform a small section of the song, thereby reducing the mammoth length of the original by approximately four minutes. The song featured in the movie during a funeral scene; the main characters sing it at their friend's grave side, in front of the dead man's unamused family. The single version then appeared during the end credits.

The song was accompanied by a video showing Madonna wearing a simple outfit of jeans and a vest top (though she did glam it up by including a tiara on her head), dancing in front of a huge American flag. It was interspersed with clips of various "regular" American citizens, and topped off with Rupert Everett dancing along with Madonna and bouncing her on his knee.

"American Pie" reached number one in the UK and many other countries, but Madonna was still not entirely sure she should have recorded it. When a record executive insisted it appear as a bonus track on her next album – *Music* – she retaliated by leaving it off *GHV2* (Greatest Hits Volume 2), claiming she was "punishing" it for having made it onto the *Music* album without her approval. It was eventually forgiven, however, and the video at least was allowed a place on the 2009 *Celebration* DVD, though not the album.

This photo shows Madonna and Rupert Everett in a still from the video.

Madonna discovered she was pregnant with her second child in early 2000, and while she chose to keep the news between herself and partner Guy Ritchie at first, it wasn't long before the media were speculating about the forthcoming happy event. She was on the promotional tour for *The Next Best Thing* at the time, and some interviewers made a point of asking if she'd like to expand her family. Each question was met by the answer that she would like to have another baby, but did not know when it would happen. Finally, however, in late March she released a statement which said she was "happy to confirm rumours" but asked for privacy from the media.

In May, Madonna made an appearance with Ritchie at the opening of the Sanderson Hotel, where she was photographed with a significant bump in a tight red-and-black dress. She is seen here with her partner Ritchie and hotelier Ian Schrager.

The US premiere of *The Next Best Thing* took place in New York in March 2000, before any announcement of Madonna's pregnancy had been confirmed. When asked by a reporter if there was to be some happy news, the singer's publicist, Liz Rosenberg, immediately tried to stop the question, while the star herself smiled and exclaimed, "There's nothing to tell."

However, by the time the London premiere arrived in July 2000, there were no such questions. The heavily pregnant Madonna arrived dressed all in black, laughing that it was the only colour that didn't make her look like a sofa. However, the media's eyes were all on television presenter Paula Yates, who walked down the red carpet looking extremely dishevelled, leading some to speculate on the state of her health. Two months later she was found dead in her London home, the victim of a heroin overdose.

This photo shows Madonna after the premiere, leaving the Ritz Hotel where she had enjoyed a meal with partner Guy Ritchie.

The Next Best Thing met with negative reactions after it was released, but this seems to have been down to a fault with the marketing campaign, which placed it in the comedy genre (some publicity even went so far as describing it as a "screwball comedy"). The film – while amusing in places – is most definitely not a funny one, and had it been classed as a drama, it may have had more of a positive reaction. Madonna's portrayal of yoga teacher Abbie is very well played and is probably the second-best performance of her life so far, next to 1996's *Evita*. It should be noted that, while the screen friendship between Madonna and Rupert Everett was also played out off-screen, it too seemed to be strained when Rupert wrote about his co-star in the 2006 book *Red Carpets and Other Banana Skins*.

This photo shows Madonna and Benjamin Bratt during a courtroom scene in the movie.

Although Madonna had been residing for the most part in England, towards the end of her pregnancy she flew back to the USA in order to give birth to her son. The singer was booked in for a C-section in the first week of September, but on 11 August these plans were changed when baby Rocco Ritchie was delivered four weeks early. Many rumours circulated that when the singer went into labour, she collapsed and was carried into the hospital by Guy Ritchie, shouting for help. Madonna later told *US Weekly* that it wasn't as dramatic as everyone had made it out to be, and Ritchie actually met her at the hospital. "He likes to think he carried me inside," she joked.

The baby was placed in intensive care and had to stay in hospital for several days after Madonna had been discharged. Every day she would travel to the hospital to visit with and feed her son, but on her forty-second birthday, Rocco was given the all-clear and was able to go home with his family.

This photo shows Madonna towards the end of her pregnancy, enjoying a day out in London.

Madonna's next album was *Music*, released in September 2000. It boasted a number of songs written about her family, including "I Deserve It", which was about her marriage to Guy Ritchie. While the music – with the possible exception of "Don't Tell Me" – couldn't really be described as country and western, Madonna's image very much was, and she wore a selection of cowboy outfits and hats for part of the promotion.

The album included a selection of thought-provoking songs, including the ballad "Gone" and the haunting "Paradise (Not for Me)", while also showcasing some electronic-filled tracks such as "Impressive Instant" and "Nobody's Perfect". There were also videos to accompany each single, including the western-themed "Don't Tell Me" and the fun-filled, pimp-style promo for the song "Music", which showed Madonna partying in a limo with friends including Debi Mazar. Also present in the clip was comedian Sacha Baron Cohen, who played her rather cheeky and innuendo-filled driver.

This photo shows Madonna in the cowboy style she sported for much of the promotion for the *Music* album.

To celebrate the release of *Music*, Madonna performed a special mini-concert for fans at Brixton Academy, London, in November 2000. This was the first live concert in the UK since *The Girlie Show*, and as a result, fans flocked to win tickets in what *NME* magazine described as the biggest scrum "since Willy Wonka threw open his gates".

Just three months after the birth of Rocco, the singer was back in shape wearing a vest top with his name blazoned across the front. She then wowed fans with six songs – "Impressive Instant", "Don't Tell Me", "Music", "Runaway Lover", "What it Feels Like for a Girl" and "Holiday". The biggest cheer went up for "Holiday", of course, and some complained afterwards that the singer should have played more of her older material. The fact that she was showcasing her new album – and therefore new songs – seemed to be completely lost on them.

For those who were unable to attend the event, they had the opportunity to listen online when the concert was broadcast live around the world. This photo shows Madonna in action, during the Brixton appearance.

Eager to try all things British, including old-fashioned pubs and Timothy Taylor beer, Madonna bought a country house in England and decided to try her hand at clay pigeon shooting. Towards the end of 2000, she bought a host of shooting outfits and paraphernalia and began taking lessons in the sport at a local shooting school. The interest caused barely a stir until it was later revealed that as well as clay pigeons (which are in fact discs of clay), the singer and her husband had also begun shooting pheasants at their country retreat.

Animal rights activists were incensed, and even though Madonna quickly explained that the birds were being shot for food, the media coverage was anything but positive.

Madonna continued to shoot pheasants for several years, until one day she watched a bird die in front of her. The realisation that the bird had suffered because of her actions was said to have prevented her from wanting to pick up a rifle again.

This photo shows the singer taking lessons in clay pigeon shooting, during winter 2000.

In December 2000, Madonna, Guy, Lourdes, Rocco and a variety of friends and family travelled to the quiet town of Dornoch in Scotland to celebrate a much-anticipated marriage and christening. As the family stepped from their private jet, a lone piper played on the runway, and this set the tone for the next few days, with a very Scottish theme at Skibo Castle, where the wedding between Madonna and Guy was to take place.

Before the big day came the christening of Rocco Ritchie, which happened on 21 December at Dornoch Cathedral. Crowds gathered outside to catch a glimpse of the famous and infamous, while one enterprising soul decided to go one better and hide himself in the organ in order to film the entire event.

For twenty-four hours the man lived, ate and slept in the instrument, and as baby Rocco was christened and Sting sang "Ave Maria" to the delighted congregation, the man got everything on tape. Sadly for him, however, thirty minutes after the ceremony one of Madonna's security team caught him carrying a rucksack and stopped to ask what he was doing. His bag was searched and inside they found the tape, along with various food items and bags of excrement. The would-be filmmaker was quickly reprimanded and the tape subsequently destroyed.

The day after Rocco's christening, Madonna dressed herself in a beautiful gown, complete with long veil and tiara. This outfit had been designed especially for her by Stella McCartney, who also apparently acted as Maid of Honour. The groom wore a kilt, as did four-month-old Rocco, while flower-girl Lourdes stood proudly next to her mother wearing a long, ivory dress.

While there was an official photographer, no guests were allowed to bring cameras into the venue, and no magazine deal was made. Madonna decided very early on that her photos would be a private affair and, quite miraculously, none were leaked at all. However, several years later an interior designer somehow got access to the couple's wedding album and apparently copied several dozen photos from it. He held on to them until 2008, when they were sold to a national newspaper, much to Madonna's chagrin. She sued, and the newspaper paid an undisclosed amount, which she donated to her Raising Malawi charity in 2009.

This photo shows Madonna and Guy leaving Scotland on the day after their wedding.

During the early days of their marriage, Madonna and Guy Ritchie made no secret of their desire to work together. Their first project came when Guy was approached by BMW to direct one of a series of mini-movies for the company, and his wife decided to take part too.

The resulting film – *Star* – saw Madonna in the title role, with actor Clive Owen as her driver. The story revolved around a spoiled woman, who at one stage wants Owen to drive her to the venue where she is to make an appearance that evening. She is so rude that he decides to have some fun at her expense, driving erratically and throwing her around on the back seat, forcing her to spill coffee all over her lap. When the star is unceremoniously dumped out of the car at the end of the film, she is seen lying on the ground, surrounded by photographers, with a big wet patch on her groin.

This photo shows Madonna and Guy shortly before they began working on the project, at the premiere party for his movie *Snatch*. They are accompanied by director Quentin Tarantino.

While there were scenes in the 2000 "Music" video that caused a certain amount of scandal – mainly when the girls visited a strip club – even more controversy came with the video that accompanied 2001's "What It Feels Like for a Girl". The video was directed by Guy Ritchie and features a remixed version of the single, along with scenes showing Madonna driving around town with an old lady as her companion. This would be innocent enough if not for the fact that the duo then go on a spree of violence, which results in Madonna slamming her car into a pole at great speed. The video was not well received by television stations; it was banned, prompting the singer to release it as a DVD single in spring 2001.

This photo shows Madonna and Guy at the 2001 Grammy Awards, around the time the video was made, with the singer sporting the same hairstyle as the one she wore in the promo.

The *Drowned World Tour*, Madonna's first trip on the road for eight years, kicked off in Barcelona, Spain, on 9 June 2001, and finished three months later, on 15 September in Los Angeles. The tour was the first she had embarked on since becoming a mother, and on many occasions both Lourdes and Rocco were spotted in a special section, with Rocco wearing mini ear protectors and Lourdes copying every move her mother made on stage.

The show itself was spectacular, with special effects such as Madonna flying across stage during an energetic rendition of "Sky Fits Heaven" and riding a mechanical bull during "Human Nature". But the concert also had a stripped-down, simple feel to it too, including a beautiful rendition of "Gone", with Madonna wearing jeans and a simple vest top. Also present was "I Deserve It", in which Madonna strummed a guitar whilst sitting on a hay bale, as seen in this photo.

On 11 September 2001, Madonna was scheduled to play at the Staples Center in Los Angeles, but it was postponed after the atrocities that took place in New York that morning. The singer returned to the stage on 13 September, but she cut several performances and songs that were no longer deemed appropriate, and gave an emotional speech which saw many people – including Madonna herself – wiping away tears from their eyes.

However, this "show must go on" attitude irked some people, especially since many other events that week had been cancelled and most of the flights were grounded. Even Madonna's official fan club magazine took a swipe at her in their next issue, though her publicist – on the outside at least – condoned her client's decision to carry on. Finally, on 15 September, the singer wrapped up the tour with the concert in Los Angeles that had originally been planned for the 11th.

After being on the road for three months, Madonna could have been forgiven for taking a rest, but instead she flew almost straight away to Europe to work with husband Guy Ritchie on their movie *Swept Away*.

This photo shows Madonna dressed in a red kilt while performing at London's Earls Court.

Probably the least successful of all Madonna's movies, *Swept Away* saw the star being directed by her husband, in what can only be described as a disappointing project. The film was a remake of the 1974 film of the same name, and Mr and Mrs Ritchie were encouraged to make it after a conversation with a friend.

Described by Madonna as a "delicious challenge", the movie was made in Malta and Sardinia and saw her in the role of Amber, a forty-year-old socialite who is both arrogant and spoiled in equal measure. During the first part of the movie she is seen tormenting Giuseppe (played by Adriano Giannini), the first mate of a yacht (actually a converted fishing boat) which Amber and her husband have rented for the summer.

An unfortunate event causes the two enemies to become shipwrecked on a desert island, where against all odds, they quickly fall in love. While the idea of the movie was good enough, the fast-moving romance between two people who had previously hated each other resulted in the film looking as though it was missing a middle section. Fans complained that the love between the two just didn't make sense and that perhaps if there had been more of a build-up, it would have been easier to understand and believe.

Swept Away went straight to DVD in the UK and has been nominated for several "bad movie" awards since. This photo shows Madonna and Giannini in a publicity still for the film.

In December 2001, shortly after releasing her next volume of greatest hits, entitled *GHV2*, Madonna was asked to present the Turner Prize at London's Tate Britain. The award was being broadcast live on UK television, and as a result, Channel 4 apparently asked the singer for a copy of her speech before the event. Madonna later told NBC that she refused to hand it over, so the people concerned tried to find out what she was going to say in various different ways. According to the singer, they also balked at the idea of introducing her as Mrs Ritchie, something she took great offence to.

Finally, after being told that there should be no profanity anywhere in the speech, Madonna took to the stage and – of course – swore at the earliest possibility, ending her appearance with the words "Right on, motherfucker – everyone is a winner". During the speech the angry star also described award shows as "silly" and declared, "The name is Mrs Ritchie, thank you very much." Afterwards, Channel 4 received complaints about the language and the channel was forced to issue an apology. Madonna meanwhile said that swearing had made her feel better about the whole debacle.

This photo shows the singer giving her controversial speech.

Madonna has always been a fan of art, and has invested in many pieces over the years, including several portraits by her favourite artist, Frida Kahlo. Two of her Kahlo paintings – *My Birth* and *Self-Portrait with Monkey* – were loaned to the Tate museum in London during 2005, and at one point she wanted very much to play the artist in a movie.

During her time in London, Madonna has been known to quietly frequent museums and galleries, so it came as no surprise for her to be seen at the National Portrait Gallery in January 2002. This time she was very much in the spotlight, however, and came in support of their Mario Testino Portraits Show, which was being held there at the time.

Accompanied by Guy and Lourdes, a conservatively dressed Madonna can be seen here with a very happy Mario Testino, the star of the show. Others in attendance that night included friend Gwyneth Paltrow, model Kate Moss and *Vogue* editor Anna Wintour.

Jean Paul Gaultier has designed outfits for Madonna ever since the 1990s, when he came up with the now-infamous cone bra for the *Blond Ambition* tour. The two have remained firm friends and are often seen together at shows, parties and events. In 2010 he spoke to *The Times* about his experiences with the singer, saying that he first met her after a 1987 concert. He later offered to make costumes for her next tour, but when she rang to take him up on the offer, he did not believe it was her. "I'm like, 'Yeah, yeah, okay, whatever.' I don't believe it's possible." But it really was Madonna on the telephone and after calling her back, the rest – as they say – is history. In 2012 Gaultier reworked the cone bra look for the singer's *MDNA* tour, thereby cementing their working relationship for some considerable time to come.

This unusual and informal photograph, taken circa 2002, shows the couple enjoying a laugh together as they sit outside a Paris restaurant.

On 23 May 2002, Madonna made her UK stage debut in *Up for Grabs* at the Wyndham's Theatre in London's celebrated West End. The play was not without controversy, however, with tales of backstage arguments and preview performances resulting in some critics questioning Madonna's acting skills. Added to that, when the play was first announced, there were matinee performances listed that were later cancelled because of Madonna's work on her new album, *American Life*. This decision left many fans furious and disappointed, jamming the theatre's switchboard in order to complain and request refunds on their tickets.

Thankfully, when Madonna finally walked on to the stage during the first official performance, the fans who did manage to get tickets were more than happy with the play – cheering so much that at one point the singer had to ask them to shush so that she could deliver her lines. Playing the role of a manipulative art dealer who is trying to obtain a Jackson Pollock painting, Madonna received mixed reviews from the critics, but the play was a great achievement in terms of sales and fan reaction. The theatre was packed to the rafters for the entire ten-week run, and while Madonna does not seem particularly keen to take to the boards again, the experience of *Up for Grabs* would surely make her box office gold if she decides to give it another go.

Madonna's appearance in the James Bond film *Die Another Day* was not as a sexy Bond girl or love interest, but as a tough fencing instructor called Verity who is not the least bit wowed by 007 and his charms.

She not only acted in the movie, but supplied a theme song sporting the same title as the film. In the action-packed video that accompanied it, Madonna is seen as a prisoner, being assaulted by guards, as well as playing a pair of good and evil fencing women. The clip was certainly violent and it was censored by many television channels, particularly the scenes showing the singer being slashed around the stomach and then smearing blood on the walls.

The video shoot was a very physical affair and ended with the "evil" fencer being killed by the "good" one, as well as the prisoner escaping from an electric chair. Much time and effort was put into it all, but in the end, the song was not as popular as it could have been, and has gone down in history as being viewed as one of the worst James Bond tunes of all time.

This photo shows Madonna and Guy at the London premiere of *Die Another Day*, held in November 2002. They are seen together with Pierce Brosnan, who played Bond in the movie, and his wife, Keely Shaye Smith.

Madonna

When it was announced that the Queen of England was to meet the Queen of Pop at the premiere of *Die Another Day*, the media went wild. What would they say to each other? How would they react? Everyone waited to find out.

In truth, the Queen is more used to meeting people than just about anyone, and has shaken hands with everyone from Marilyn Monroe to President Bush, so the thrill of meeting Madonna probably wasn't something that even crossed her mind. Still, the singer was excited to be introduced, and later declared that, while the two had never met before, she had surprised herself by not being at all nervous. As for what one queen said to the other, well apparently Queen Elizabeth did not know much about Madonna – some even say that she had no idea who she was – but after having it explained to her, she did show some interest in the fact that the singer had just recorded the theme song to the latest Bond movie.

This photo shows Madonna taking the Queen's hand, before lowering into a well-practised curtsy.

On the same night that she first met the Queen Madonna also encountered Prince Philip. Known for his famous faux pas with everyone from students to presidents, people must have waited with bated breath to see what he would come up with when he came face to face with the Queen of Pop.

Apparently the prince did not disappoint and after Madonna explained to him that she had written the theme for the latest James Bond film, Prince Philip was said to have gushed, "Are we going to need ear plugs?" Madonna's reaction to this loaded question remains unrecorded.

This photo shows the singer curtsying gingerly, while shaking the Prince's hand.

April 2003 saw the release of the new album *American Life*, and a completely new image to go with it. The idea behind the record came, Madonna said, when she started to look back on her career and life, and wondered whether or not various things were actually important or had made her happy in some way. She began to write down her thoughts and the result was an assortment of soul-searching and often beautiful songs, about her parents, her struggles with fame, her children, her husband and her spirituality.

The anger in some of the tracks makes it an album that the listener will either love or hate, which in turn gained mixed reviews from critics and fans alike. However, with tracks such as "Love Profusion" and "Nothing Fails", it more than deserves its place amongst the all-time great Madonna albums.

This photo shows the singer in April 2003, at the launch party for the book *72 Names of God*. She can be seen showing off her new *American Life* image.

Madonna was used to causing controversy with her videos, but the single "American Life" promised to cause more scandal than ever before. Shortly before war broke out in Iraq in 2003, the singer decided to make the video to show her thoughts on what was a very hot topic at the time. She dressed in combat gear, showed gruesome images of the casualties of war and also included a President George W. Bush lookalike.

Madonna said she hoped the video would show a different, more peaceful way of rectifying the crisis in Iraq, but by the time it was finished, the country was already at war. Suddenly it didn't seem like the right time to release the promo, and after thinking about the way it may affect her daughter at school and her husband at work, Madonna did something she had never done before: she pulled the existing video and replaced it with a more toned-down, less controversial version.

This photo shows a publicity photo for the "American Life" video.

Madonna

With the release of the *American Life* album, the newly-brunette star took part in many TV specials around the world, including an in-depth interview with Megan Mullally. During the chat, the two talked about various aspects of their lives, including Madonna's appearance in Megan's comedy show, *Will and Grace*. The episode saw her playing the part of Karen's (Mullally) new roommate and was extremely funny, showing a side to Madonna that perhaps some did not know existed; that of being able to make fun of herself.

Other stops on the publicity tour included a chat on the *Live with Regis and Kelly* show in the USA, and then on *The Jonathan Ross Show* in the UK. The latter had spoken to Madonna during the infamous *Sex* era in 1992, but this time the talk was very different and focused on her work, children and life in England.

This photo shows a happy Madonna, when she appeared during the tour with interviewer Oliver Geissen. She had just taped a show called *Absolut Madonna*, which aired in Germany during April 2003.

Madonna has looked to the classic stars for inspiration in her work throughout her career, and this was particularly apparent in the video for the 2003 single "Hollywood". The clip was a definite tribute to stars gone by, as well as presenting some of the agonies involved in becoming camera ready, such as Botox and hair styling. The video showed the singer in various guises, including a vamp in a black curly wig and bright red lipstick, and then a red-headed 1930s lady, cavorting in satin pyjamas in front of an array of mirrors. But perhaps the most "Hollywood" of all the looks was as a blonde, Jean Harlow/Thelma

Todd lookalike, sitting astride an old-fashioned television set and teasing a young woman dressed as a maid.

The video was a complete departure from the anger of the "American Life" promo, and became a hit with fans, though not so with the son of French fashion photographer Guy Bourdin, who apparently complained that the looks presented were extremely similar to his father's work. The matter was eventually settled, though details of the agreement between the photographer's estate and Madonna have been kept confidential.

While Missy Elliott and Madonna may not seem at first like the most natural of partners, in summer 2003 they teamed up to present a campaign for clothes retailer Gap. The project consisted of a series of print adverts and displays, showing the singers modelling their jeans. The television commercial, meanwhile, included a remixed version of the singles "Hollywood" and "Into the Groove", and presented a Gap-related rap by Missy herself. The two were once again seen wearing the jeans collection, and the commercial showed them dancing together while walking through a Hollywood back lot.

Afterwards, Madonna released a short album called *Remixed and Revisited*, which included various reworked tracks, including the song featured in the Gap commercial, as well as a new song called "Your Honesty". Madonna later appeared as a mentor on Missy's show, *Road to Stardom with Missy Elliott*, in 2005. "Madonna is an icon in this business," Missy explained. "If anybody can give words of wisdom, it would be Madonna."

This photo shows Madonna with Missy Elliott, at a party in Los Angeles in 2004.

When Madonna agreed to take part in the 2003 MTV awards, little did anyone know that the performance would be talked about for even longer than her first appearance in 1984. The segment began with flower girls (including daughter Lourdes) taking to the stage to scatter petals. Shortly after, singer Britney Spears appeared on top of a wedding cake, singing "Like a Virgin" in an outfit similar to the one Madonna had originally worn.

By the time she reached the bottom, she had been joined by Christina Aguilera, wearing a similar costume, before finally Madonna appeared as a groom, complete with top hat and tails. Singing "Hollywood", she strutted down the stage, dancing with Britney and Christina as her two "brides". However, it was towards the end of the song when controversy came, as she suddenly kissed Britney and then Christina, before introducing Missy Elliott to the stage.

The audience loved it and afterwards the newspapers were filled with stories about the open-mouthed kiss shared between Madonna and Britney, but not much seemed to be said about her embrace with Christina. This photo, therefore, is chosen to redress the balance.

It is interesting to note that during time spent with Britney before the performance, the young singer asked Madonna to work with her on a song. She agreed and the result was called "Me Against the Music" which featured on Britney's album *In the Zone*.

In summer 2003, Madonna announced her intention to publish a variety of children's books, inspired by the teachings of Kabbalah. The first, *The English Roses* (published in September of that year), was inspired by a group of girls at her daughter's school, who were given the nickname by a teacher. The girls provided inspiration for the name, but the bulk of the story seems to have come from Madonna's feelings of abandonment and of not fitting in after the death of her mother.

The main character, Bina, is a young girl who seems to have it all; hence she is ignored by the "English Roses" and is excluded from their games, picnics and dances. One evening a crotchety fairy godmother arrives to show the girls that, while they may think Bina has it all, actually she spends all her time looking after her father and lamenting the loss of her mother. The girls then feel awful for the way they have treated her, and they all later become firm friends.

The book was lavishly illustrated by Jeffrey Fulvimari and garnered several follow-up stories, including *Too Good to be True* and *Goodbye Grace?* Over ten years on, *The English Roses* is still popular with children, and continues to sell.

This photo shows Madonna and daughter Lourdes, during a reading of the book at Kensington Roof Gardens, in September 2003.

2004 saw the first Madonna tour for three years, and came in the shape of *Re-Invention*, a word constantly attributed to the singer thanks to her ever-changing image. Beginning in May and ending in September, the show concentrated mainly in the USA, with other stops including England, Ireland, Paris, the Netherlands and Portugal. Cramming in over twenty songs, the concert included "re-invented" renditions of Madonna's most popular songs, including "Vogue", "Material Girl", "Into the Groove", "Papa Don't Preach" and "Holiday". Within this were different themes and segments inspired by Marie Antoinette, Military, Circus, Acoustic and Scottish Tribal.

When Madonna came on to the stage, she did so while practising a series of advanced yoga postures, before entering into a lively version of "Vogue" and then "Nobody Knows Me", performed on a moving platform. A darker theme was explored when "American Life" was performed, but then it was all change during a rock-based, guitar-blasting rendition of "Material Girl".

This photo shows Madonna whilst performing at Earls Court, London.

The second part of the *Re-Invention* concert came in the shape of a dance interlude featuring "Hollywood", before Madonna returned to the stage with an energetic, circus-themed "Hanky Panky". "Nothing Fails", "Don't Tell Me", "Like a Prayer", "Mother and Father" and John Lennon's "Imagine" were all performed, before finally things became upbeat in the Scottish section, which included "Into the Groove" and "Papa Don't Preach".

The finale of *Re-Invention* was all about "Music" and "Holiday", then finally it was all over when the curtain came down to reveal the words "Re-invent Yourself" and Madonna bid the crowd goodnight.

In all, the show was extremely popular; remixes of her major songs proved to be a well-received tribute to her career, and showed just how much Madonna had grown as an artist. It has never been released on official DVD, though parts of it were shown in the *I Want to Tell You a Secret* movie, released in 2005.

This photo shows Madonna re-inventing her 1986 "Italians Do It Better" T-shirt into one with a "Kabbalists Do It Better" motto.

In September 2004, at the end of the *Re-Invention* tour, Madonna announced that she was heading to Israel to take part in various events linked to the Jewish New Year. During several days, Madonna met up with 2,000 other Kabbalah followers and also found time for some private visits too, although she became frustrated when her car was surrounded by fans whenever she attempted to leave the hotel.

Perhaps the best moment for many was when Madonna took to the stage during a children's programme, in order to talk to the crowd of delegates. During her speech she described being initially nervous about travelling to Israel, but in the end felt it to be no more dangerous than being in New York. She also spoke about what the Kabbalah meant to her, explaining that by studying the system, she believed it was her responsibility (and those around her) to make the world a better place.

This photo shows Madonna making her passionate speech.

After her trip to Israel, Madonna continued to study Kabbalah, and by this time had introduced husband Guy Ritchie to it as well. This was something that wasn't easy at first, thanks to the fact that he was a Darwinist who tended to avoid anything spiritual. However, Ritchie eventually began studying too, and together with his wife could be frequently seen at the Kabbalah centre, both in London and New York.

While the media were unrelenting in their criticism of Madonna's beliefs, the singer brushed off their words and continued to speak about her faith in interviews. Other followers included Demi Moore and Gwyneth Paltrow, and in October 2004 they all went to Home House in London to celebrate the launch of a Kabbalah book. Once there, the celebrities mingled with other A-list members, and listened to a speech given by the centre's co-director Michael Berg.

This photo shows Madonna at the event, with her good friend Demi Moore.

The *Adventures of Abdi* was another book in the series of children's stories that Madonna published towards the mid-2000s. This volume told the tale of a little boy who is asked to deliver a precious necklace to the queen. On the way to see her, he encounters many struggles, but no matter how hard it becomes, the boy never gives up hope that he will complete his task.

With all her books, Madonna would read what she'd written to Lourdes, and if the child became bored, it would be rewritten until she found the story interesting. The singer has always been adamant that writing children's books was never something she had thought about, and when her Kabbalah teacher suggested it, Madonna was not sold on the idea at all. However, having thought about it for a while, she decided to give it a go, and the books became extremely meaningful for her, both critically and personally.

Madonna took part in publicity for *The Adventures of Abdi* in late 2002, which included a reading for St Winifred's School pupils, at Selfridges, London. This photo shows the singer sharing a page from her book while reading to the children.

In November 2004, Madonna became a founding member of the UK Hall of Fame when she was inducted after a glowing introduction by radio DJ Jo Whiley and artist Tracey Emin. After showing a film of various personalities sharing their thoughts on the artist, Madonna finally took to the stage and accepted her award, giving thanks for her induction.

In the speech she joked that if someone had told her as a child that she would one day be married to a British man and living in England, she would have said, "Bollocks to that!" Madonna then said she liked to think the award was given more for her accomplishments than her fame, and topped it all off by declaring that she was very grateful to have finally found her voice and that, in turn, it had given others a voice too.

This photo shows Madonna giving her speech, while Jo Whiley stands behind her

UK
MUSIC
HALL
OF
FAME

While Madonna never liked London in the early days, claiming that all the phones were bugged and she had no privacy, there can be little doubt that during her marriage to Guy Ritchie she settled very well into the English lifestyle. Weekends were spent at the couple's country house, and on weekdays she would reside in a huge townhouse close to Marble Arch. It was during this time that a more down-to-earth side to Madonna began to come out. She invested in a Mini Cooper, took part in an intensive driving course to help her negotiate the new roads, and even told reporters that she was comfortable enough to help when someone stopped to ask her for directions.

She could often be seen wearing a tracksuit around town, and later laughed that Lourdes would complain and ask why she didn't dress up like other mums did while on the school run. But the natural flow of life seemed to suit Madonna, and she frequently stopped at her local pub for a half pint of ale and a packet of crisps after a hard day's work. The star was also often seen riding her bike to the gym or Kabbalah centre, as can be seen in this photo from 2005.

The friendship formed between Madonna and Rosie O'Donnell on the set of *A League of their Own* has remained strong. The two have kept in touch mainly over email in recent years, although they have also been seen together on various occasions, as can be seen in this June 2005 photograph.

The friends appeared together in an interview on *The Arsenio Hall Show* during 1992, and Rosie took part in VH1's *Madonna: Behind the Music* in 1999. Madonna seemed happy and relaxed during several appearances on Rosie's popular 1990s talk show, during which they embarrassed each other with clips of "the old days". The singer also tried – unsuccessfully – to teach the talk-show host how to practise yoga live on air, much to the amusement of the audience.

The two women spend time together socially whenever they can, and Rosie has joked that the only time Madonna's children get to watch television and eat junk food is when they visit her home.

Released in June 2005, *Lotsa De Casha* was the fifth children's book to be written by Madonna, following *The English Roses*, *Mr Peabody's Apples*, *Yakov and the Seven Thieves* and *The Adventures of Abdi*. The book told the story of a very rich greyhound who seemed to have everything he could ever wish for, but was really selfish and deeply unhappy. The book's lesson is that money cannot buy everything, and on its release it became another bestseller for the author.

Madonna took part in publicity for the release, which included posing with a man dressed as Lotsa De Casha himself, and several signings and appearances. One such event was held at the Bergdorf Goodman store in New York, where she can be seen in this picture, posing next to a stack of books and a happy young reader.

Live 8 was a concert held in London's Hyde Park on 2 July 2005 to raise awareness of extreme world hunger, and to encourage politicians to try to "make poverty history" during the upcoming G8 summit. As they had for Live Aid, Bob Geldof and Midge Ure came together to organise the concert, and acts included the likes of U2, Robbie Williams – and of course Madonna.

While the concert was a huge accomplishment, perhaps the most memorable section was during Madonna's appearance, when a young woman by the name of Birhan Woldu joined her on stage. While the name may not be familiar, most people will surely remember her appearance in videos for the original Live Aid project, a small child literally at the brink of starvation. Now a grown woman, a beautiful, smiling Birhan joined Madonna at the beginning of her time on stage, and stayed with her during much of "Like a Prayer".

After that song – and Birhan's departure – Madonna continued her segment with belting renditions of "Ray of Light" and "Music", before speaking to interviewer Jo Whiley. During the interview she spoke about her experience on stage and was asked if she would ever like to visit Africa herself. Later the star said that this conversation planted a seed and encouraged her to think seriously about how she could help African children.

This photo shows the singer and Birhan sharing a hug on stage.

On 16 August 2005, Madonna decided to celebrate her birthday by going horse riding with friends. However, it didn't all go to plan, as she was asked to ride a polo horse that she had never ridden before. Suddenly the animal became spooked by something and the singer ended up falling off its back. At first she thought there was nothing wrong and tried to stand up, but, in Madonna's words, her skeleton then collapsed and she found herself passed out on the floor.

When the singer was taken to hospital, it was discovered that she had broken eight bones in various parts of her body, including her collar bone, scapula, ribs and knuckle. Madonna was not a good patient by her own admission, and when the doctor told her she was going to be house-bound for the foreseeable future, she was furious. However, the one person who was happy that she had to stop working was daughter Lourdes, who celebrated the fact that her mother would be spending more time with her over the next few weeks.

This photo shows a fragile Madonna, arriving at the Kabbalah centre during her recovery from the accident.

Guy Ritchie's movie *Revolver* was released to a European audience in September 2005. Though still recovering from her recent riding accident, Madonna attended the premiere with her husband, her hair straight against her face and arm in a sling. Obviously still in a lot of pain, the singer's mood did not seem particularly upbeat on the red carpet, and she rarely managed much of a smile. When asked what she thought about the violence portrayed in the movie, Madonna declared that there was no way she would want her son or daughter to watch it. "It is very violent," she said. "But I think it reflects the violence of the world we live in."

This photo shows Guy kissing Madonna's forehead at the premiere party, held at Waxy O'Connor's in London. Her black sling can be seen clearly in the shot.

In October 2005, when promoting her upcoming *Confessions on a Dance Floor* album, Madonna appeared once again on David Letterman's show in New York. During the interview, she spoke about her life in England, and in particular her country pile in Wiltshire, discussing her love of feeding the chickens and her refusal to let her children watch television. Letterman has a knack of putting Madonna at ease due to his fun-poking ways, and as a result the interview was a relaxed and informal event.

One thing Madonna did mention was that her record company were very much against her getting back on a horse until the promotion of her album was finished. However, after seeing several horses outside the television studio, she agreed to ride for the first time since the accident. Looking rather nervous at first, she was seen being led slowly down the street, though things threatened to turn nasty when Letterman's horse seemed to get rather jittery. However, the ride was soon over without incident, much to the relief of Madonna and – it can be guessed – her record company.

Autumn 2005 saw the release of the new album *Confessions on a Dance Floor*, and the single "Hung Up". Boasting the riff from the Abba song "Gimme Gimme Gimme", "Hung Up" was an up-tempo track that set the tone for the rest of the album: all disco numbers with no ballads anywhere in sight. Also, each track was mixed seamlessly into the next, so that one could dance to the whole album without stopping.

The clever thing about the album was that, while each song had a disco feel with an electronic sound, the lyrics were very confessional and seemed to say a lot about Madonna's thoughts on life, marriage and everything in between. Listened to on the surface, it is a perfectly happy, feel-good album, but bubbling underneath is the idea that you can be confessional without being maudlin.

The video for "Hung Up" saw Madonna in a dance studio, practising her moves, before heading out to the street and mingling with her dancers, and finally finding her way to an arcade in order to continue the moves on a dance machine. It was all filmed just months after her riding accident, but she still put everything into the video, despite later revealing that she had been in a huge amount of pain.

This photo shows the singer at London's Koko Club, looking just like she did in the "Hung Up" video.

Madonna

I'm Going to Tell You a Secret is a
2005 documentary focused on the
Re-Invention tour of the year before.
The film was a follow-up to 1991's
Truth or Dare, but this time showed
how much Madonna had grown, both
emotionally and spiritually, during
the years that had passed. The film's
co-stars were her husband, children
and various members of cast and
crew, and together they revealed sides
of the singer not frequently shown,
including scenes where she chats to
her daughter in French, and jokingly
bickers with her husband.

Shot mainly in black and white,
I'm Going to Tell You a Secret followed
the star around the world, taking in
everywhere from Hollywood to Paris
and even her hometown of Detroit.

During that section of the film, she is
seen spending time with her father
and step-mother, as well as showing
a glimpse of their countryside Ciccone
vineyard.

One of the appearances Madonna
made in support of _I'm Going to Tell
You a Secret_ came when she attended
Hunter College and gave a speech
about her life, as well as answering
questions from the surprised students.
When talking about her journey she
said, "Once you start to learn, you
understand that you know nothing, and
there's so much more to learn; and it's
a very humbling experience."

This photo shows Madonna at the
film's London premiere, in November
2005.

In November 2005, Madonna agreed to help turn on the Christmas lights at her friend Stella McCartney's London shop. Wearing a large coat and her *Confessions* hairstyle, the singer laughed and joked with David Walliams and Matt Lucas from comedy show *Little Britain*. They then had rather a relaxed chat with her afterwards, during which they spoke about Madonna's recent appearances on several UK chat shows.

Later, Walliams said that he and Lucas received a phone call from Madonna's assistant shortly after the meeting, asking them to join the singer for dinner. They agreed, but just moments before they were supposed to go, they received another call, this time telling them that Madonna may not be there after all, as she was just in from a busy day and was extremely tired. Not wishing to risk having to sit in a restaurant waiting to see if the star would show up or not, the duo decided to cancel the entire affair, and it is not known if the meeting was ever rescheduled.

This photo shows Madonna sharing a joke with Stella McCartney and David Walliams (dressed as a character from *Little Britain*), during the Christmas switch-on.

In February 2006, Madonna won the award for Best International Female Solo Artist at the Brit Awards. However, while the award was celebrated by fans, it was the state of the singer's marriage that caused the most press coverage. Shortly before the event, it had been noted that Guy had not appeared with Madonna when she attended the Grammy Awards in the US, and while he joked that he had to stay home to look after the children, the newspapers were full of speculation that the marriage was failing.

Ritchie did accompany his wife to the Brits, but this didn't stop gossips from putting pen to paper when the singer was photographed without her wedding ring. Furthermore, when told she had won the award, the kiss she shared with her husband was a decidedly awkward one on the cheek. Then, giving her speech, Ritchie was not mentioned. Instead Madonna thanked British artists and producers for inspiration, and her UK fans, "Because without you I'd just be another singer across the pond."

This photo shows Madonna at the press call, after winning her award.

While Madonna loves to dress up, she certainly knows how to dress down too, as can be seen here, in this photograph for the *W* magazine pre-Oscar retreat party in March 2006. Sporting a woolly hat and a vest top with the motif "Queen of the Dance Floor", the singer is seen with dress designer and friend Arianne Phillips.

Phillips has been a huge presence in Madonna's life, working with her since the mid-1990s, and has designed costumes for five of her concert tours, as well as for films *Swept Away* and

W.E. For the latter, she won various accolades for her work, including an Academy Award nomination. This was little wonder, as the designer began researching for the movie a full year before shooting was due to begin, and the costumes she came up with were nothing short of spectacular.

The two women work extremely well together and Phillips has credited Madonna with encouraging her to push herself, therefore making her a better artist.

While Madonna has never been nominated for an Oscar, she has continually supported the Academy by appearing and sometimes performing at the ceremony. In recent years she has also begun hosting an after-party, where the winners – and losers – can celebrate or commiserate together. Her events – sometimes hosted with Demi Moore, and at other times with her manager Guy Oseary – have become increasingly popular with the big names, all eager to attend due to the strictly private and intimate nature of the evening.

Still, while Madonna may enjoy playing the hostess, she also likes attending other people's Oscar parties too, such as the *Vanity Fair* event, which is always seen as a rival to her own. She has been seen frequently at the party over the years, including when this photo was taken, in 2006.

May 2006 saw Madonna back on the road with the *Confessions* tour, which went around the world until late September. The concert showcased the *Confessions on a Dance Floor* album, along with a variety of older tracks such as "Like a Virgin", "Live To Tell" and "La Isla Bonita". It also sported four different themes: Equestrian, Bedouin, Glam-Punk and Disco.

It was during the *Confessions* tour that the star had her most glamorous entrance, in the shape of a disco ball which opened to reveal Madonna singing "Future Lovers", before launching into "Get Together" and then "Like a Virgin". This particular song had a nod to her 2005 riding accident, with a screen showing X-rays of broken bones while Madonna rode on something that resembled a cross between a mechanical horse and a carousel ride.

This photo shows Madonna looking rather regal, during the equestrian section of a concert in Rome, Italy.

One of the most controversial parts of the *Confessions* show came when Madonna appeared on stage singing "Live to Tell" whilst hanging from a disco-themed cross and sporting a crown of thorns on her head. It goes without saying that this angered various religious groups, and several even threatened to sue her for blasphemy. The furore was so bad that Madonna later released a statement saying that she was not mocking the church; that her performance was no different from her wearing a cross around her neck and she was not blasphemous. "Rather it is my plea to the audience to encourage mankind to help one another and to see the world as a unified whole," she explained.

While this part of the show caused many an eyebrow to be raised, the latter half was back to being up-tempo, with a celebration of disco and glam-punk. The finale of "Lucky Star" and "Hung Up" was very popular, and included Madonna in full-on disco gear, while several dancers jumped their way around the audience.

This photo shows Madonna on the cross, during the most controversial part of the show.

While Madonna may not (yet) have had the privilege of leaving her hand and foot prints at the famous Mann's Chinese Theatre in Los Angeles, she did become the first person to leave a bronze impression of her hands outside Wembley Arena, London. The extraordinary deed was completed in August 2006, when she was invited to begin the Square of Fame, and she was only too happy to oblige.

After pressing her hands into the mould in front of cheering fans, the singer told reporters that she was honoured to have been asked to do it. "I did it because it makes me feel like an honorary Brit", she said, before being presented with a plaque for herself and then heading to rehearsals for her forthcoming Wembley concert.

This photo shows Madonna placing her hands into the bronze mould, in what can only be described as a double-jointed position.

Madonna first became involved with the plight of children in Malawi after receiving a phone call from a businesswoman desperate to raise awareness for the country. At the time, the singer did not know anything about Malawi at all and could not pinpoint it on a map. This was said to have angered the fundraiser, who apparently slammed down the phone on the surprised star. But while the phone call may have seemed fruitless at the time, it actually piqued Madonna's attention and interest, and after spending some years doing research, she found herself travelling to the country in the latter part of 2006.

The trip was confusing for the singer because, while seeing an enormous amount of suffering, she also became aware that there was a great deal of love and hope with the people who lived there. She immediately started to think that perhaps she could make a difference, and the first way of doing that was to set up a charity. Later, she would adopt a child herself. For some years, Madonna and Guy had made no secret of their desire to expand their family, and meeting a baby boy called David Banda cemented their thoughts that perhaps this was one way they could help – by saving the life of a child.

This photo shows David arriving in London in the arms of Madonna's assistant, in October 2006.

When Madonna first met David in the orphanage, he was extremely ill with pneumonia, and had apparently survived malaria and tuberculosis. She was terrified to leave the youngster in that condition, and persuaded the orphanage to allow her to take him to the hospital for treatment. This eventually led to an official application to adopt the child, which the media made a huge issue of thanks to the fact that David already had a father (his mother had died in childbirth). According to Madonna, Yohane Banda had not seen his son in some time, and when she met the man in the courthouse, she explained that if he liked, she would pay for him to look after David by himself and keep him in Malawi. The father said no, he did not wish that to happen, and after a while gave his approval of the adoption, on the condition that she would bring the child back to see him in the future. Madonna agreed.

After working their way through various rounds of red tape, Madonna and Guy were allowed to arrange for the child to travel to England in order to start a new life. This was to be first as their long-term foster child, and then – as soon as the courts allowed – as their adopted son.

This photo shows David shortly after his arrival in London, in the arms of his mother.

Madonna's adoption of David Banda caused an outrage among various groups, newspapers and do-gooders, with some falsely claiming that she had stolen a child from Malawi, or used her money to fast-track the adoption in some way. The media outcry seemed as though it would never die down, and reporters even found their way to David's father and took it upon themselves to report that, despite what he may have said in court, he was not happy with the adoption.

Finally, in order to defend her decision to adopt the boy, Madonna agreed to appear on several news shows, including a special BBC television programme and an episode of *Oprah* in the USA. This photo shows the star talking to Oprah about her decision to adopt, during which time she declared that the media outrage was doing a huge injustice to the children of Malawi by making prospective parents wary of trying to adopt there. She told the interviewer that David had fitted into her family straight away, and that her other children never once had asked why he was there, or why his skin colour was different to their own. "My only thinking was that I wanted to open up my home ... To give a life to a child who otherwise would not have had one," she said.

VIA SATELLITE
MADONNA
LONDON

In December 2006, shortly after weathering the brouhaha surrounding David Banda's adoption, Madonna attended the British Comedy Awards. Once there she took to the stage in order to present the Ronnie Barker Award to Sacha Baron Cohen for his movie *Borat*.

Jonathan Ross introduced Madonna, and after walking to the podium, she received a great deal of praise and applause from the audience. Ross then declared that it had been an extraordinary year for the star, congratulating her on the tour and "on your lovely little black baby, David". The comment was certainly near the knuckle, and when he quipped that the only thing he'd come back from Africa with was a wallet, Madonna immediately retorted, "Well you might go home with a black eye." Ross then accepted defeat and the audience cheered her quick-thinking remark.

This photo shows Madonna and Jonathan Ross on stage.

Premiered in the UK during January 2007, *Arthur and the Invisibles* is a children's movie, boasting both live-action and animation. The film tells the story of a young boy called Arthur (played by Freddie Highmore) and the adventures he has while trying to find some rubies protected by tiny creatures living in his grandparents' garden. Following on from her work in children's literature, Madonna was happy to take on the voice of Princess Selenia, and together with Arthur (who has shrunk to a tiny size), she must help protect their land from an evil wizard, played by David Bowie.

Madonna arrived at the London premiere with not only her husband, but children Lourdes and Rocco too. While they seemed excited about seeing the movie, sadly the critics weren't so enthralled, and gave it decidedly mixed or negative reviews. That said, the film was eventually followed by a sequel, though Madonna did not take part and Selenia was voiced by Selena Gomez instead.

This photo shows Madonna with director Luc Besson and actor Freddie Highmore, inside the theatre at the London premiere.

In February 2007 it was announced that Madonna had designed a collection of clothes to be sold in branches of high-street giant H&M. Entitled M by Madonna, the collection included dresses, coats, bags and sunglasses among other things, all put together with designer Margareta van den Bosch. The collection was said to reflect Madonna's unique style, and the singer herself was extremely pleased with the result.

When the range was released, the public went wild. Fans crowded into Oxford Street, London, in order to buy up everything they could, with women purchasing goods to wear, and some men buying purely because they wanted to own something Madonna had designed. The collection was popular, and while she has not gone on to design anything for H&M recently, the experience was obviously a good one, as she later supported her daughter, Lourdes, when she released her Material Girl range.

This photo shows Madonna wearing a white dress from the collection, at the Langham Hotel, London.

The H&M campaign was accompanied by a number of publicity photos showing Madonna modelling numerous outfits from the collection. The pictures were shown in various magazines and on billboards across the world, spreading the look of the outfits far and wide.

There was also a television advertisement to publicise the collection, showing not only parts of the range, but also Madonna's sense of humour and acquired British accent. The advert begins with a young fashion reject coming into an office occupied by Madonna, playing an Anna Wintour-type fashion icon. There then follows scenes of the singer and entourage trying to figure out what fashion is, before finally the young girl at the beginning of the advert is transformed into a woman trendy enough to link arms with Madonna herself.

This photo shows the singer wearing an H&M dress, projected onto the wall of the Roosevelt Hotel, Hollywood.

After causing controversy over the adoption of David Banda in 2006, Madonna returned to Malawi in April of the following year. This time she was accompanied by her baby and daughter Lourdes in order to visit schools and orphanages, including the one David had been adopted from. Lourdes took a great interest in the trip and spent a lot of time working with small babies in various care centres. Madonna later said that her daughter was "amazing" and that she had grown up before her very eyes whilst working eight hours a day in the voluntary job.

Shortly after the trip, the singer gave an interview to *Vanity Fair*, where she explained her motives behind the support of Malawi, and declared that she wanted to see more girls being educated in the country. "Women are the future of Africa," she said.

This photo shows Madonna holding baby David, while Lourdes teaches him to blow kisses for the photographers.

Madonna has always been interested in making movies, but as an actress rather than someone behind the camera. This all changed when she decided to direct a relatively short movie entitled *Filth and Wisdom*. The writing of the film was a long affair, mainly thanks to the fact that Madonna was working hard on other aspects of her career, so the script could only be written in short intervals. However, by the time it was finished she was completely ready for the experience, getting to the set before anyone else and making sure she was involved with every aspect of the project.

The film revolved around a cross-dressing dominatrix called AK (played by Eugene Hutz) and his two flatmates, Holly, a ballerina turned striper, and Juliette, a pharmacist who wants to help African children. The movie was shot in May 2007, with London being the location of choice.

This photo shows Madonna on the set of the movie, fully engrossed in directing. She later told reporters that the best bit about the shoot was that she did not have to get her hair and make-up done every day; something which can be seen in this particular photo.

July 2007 saw the Live Earth concert – an event designed to raise awareness of climate change – hit venues around the world, including Wembley Stadium, London. The UK concert included the likes of Genesis, Razorlight, Duran Duran, Metallica and James Blunt, but it was Madonna who stole the show when she closed the London segment with four songs: "Ray of Light", "La Isla Bonita", "Hung Up" and a brand new track, "Hey You".

The last song, written especially for the event and co-produced by Pharrell Williams, was a rather beautiful track, inspired by climate change and the Live Earth campaign itself. As she sang, photos of various world events and people were projected behind her, before a school choir broke into song half-way through the track. Madonna herself went over to join them, and delighted one student when she put a reassuring arm around her shoulders.

This photo shows the singer performing at the event.

In early September 2007, Madonna attended the *GQ* Men of the Year Awards at the Royal Opera House, London. While there, she met up with interior designer David Collins, who had been a friend of hers since the 1990s, and had at one point designed a Miami nightclub owned by friend Ingrid Casares. Collins had even gained a writing credit for Madonna's single "Drowned World/Substitute for Love" in 1998.

On 17 July 2013, just three weeks after being diagnosed with skin cancer, Collins passed away and Madonna was devastated. Taking to Facebook and Instagram, the singer posted a photo of some roses and described how the two had known each other for a long time, and that he was a great talent and a loyal friend. She then jetted to Ireland for his funeral, wearing a sombre polka-dot dress with dark glasses covering her eyes.

This photo shows the two in a shot taken at the 2007 *GQ* awards.

Taking a break from post-production of *Filth and Wisdom*, in September 2007 Madonna travelled with husband Guy Ritchie to Israel, for a Kabbalah conference held in Tel Aviv. Once there, they mingled with other delegates, including Demi Moore, Ashton Kutcher and Rosie O'Donnell, and then were spotted clapping and singing along to Jewish songs during the large get-together.

As with her 2004 visit to the country, Madonna had a huge amount of security with her, and the trip was treated as a strictly private affair with no paparazzi welcome. However, both Madonna and Guy were happy to pose for photographs with the Israeli President, Shimon Peres, who can be seen with them in this picture. The President was said to have given Madonna a copy of the Hebrew Bible, while the singer returned the favour by presenting him with an inscribed copy of the Zohar.

Since the visit, Madonna has maintained a good relationship with the country, visiting again several times and declaring her belief that Israel is the energy centre of the world. "If we can all live together in harmony in this place, then we can live in peace all over the world," she has said.

While Guy Ritchie's movie *Revolver* was premiered to a European audience in 2005, the reception was so negative that he went back into the studio and reworked the film. The result was a limited release to US theatres in December 2007.

For the US premiere, Madonna appeared with Ritchie and the two spoke candidly to reporters on the red carpet. They looked happy in each other's company; though when Madonna continually butted in to Ritchie's answers, it seemed as though there were times when he was patiently biting his tongue. At one point the reporter asked if Madonna had visited the set during production, to which she replied that she had, but not much due to the fact that the men all liked to practise their wrestling in the lunch hour. "It's a men's club," she added.

When asked what the plans for the future Christmas holiday were, Madonna said, "We're going far, far away."

This photo shows the couple looking happy and relaxed on the red carpet.

As she has grown up, Lourdes has become more and more involved with Madonna's career and is often seen with her on the red carpet, at premieres and parties. In February 2008, the eleven-year-old joined her mother at an event to raise money for UNICEF and Madonna's charity Raising Malawi. During press interviews as they arrived, Lourdes appeared shy but told reporters that she felt her mother had done a really great job with her fundraising efforts. "I'm pretty proud ... she's been stressed," she said, as Madonna laughed. The singer, meanwhile, described how she wanted to put her charity on the map; that she felt incredibly honoured to be at the event, and wanted to inspire people. "I don't want them to just write me a cheque; I want them to give me a piece of their heart."

This photo shows Madonna and Lourdes inside the United Nations headquarters in New York, where the event was held.

In March 2008, Madonna received the honour of being inducted into the Rock and Roll Hall of Fame, in New York. Given a cheeky introduction by Justin Timberlake, Madonna came onto the stage to great applause and a standing ovation. She then went on to give a speech which was incredibly personal, talking about her ballet teacher, Christopher Flynn, early boyfriend/fellow musician Dan Gilroy, and various other people who had inspired and helped her along the way.

Her talk was informative and at times very witty, and the singer came across as being greatly humbled to be honoured in such a way. She thanked many people profusely for their help in her career, including her fans. "I did not get here on my own, and why would I want to?" Madonna told the audience.

This photo shows Madonna and Justin Timberlake posing for photographers after the induction.

At this point in Madonna's life, her marriage to Guy Ritchie was unravelling, and this is apparent on *Hard Candy*, the album she released in April 2008. "Miles Away", a song about someone who prefers he and his partner to be thousands of miles apart, seems to fit this bill rather nicely, while "She's Not Me" feels like a swipe at someone desperately trying to take her place.

There are lighter moments, with the likes of "Give It 2 Me", an upbeat number with Pharrell Williams, as well as the popular "Four Minutes" with Justin Timberlake. However, the album was not a critical success. Reviewers at the time wondered if she had gone off making music, while others described the project as "lifeless" or "stale". It did reach number one in various countries around the world, but in spite of that, many fans agree that *Hard Candy* is not the best example of a classic Madonna album.

The singer is seen here during an appearance at the Roseland Ballroom, in order to publicise *Hard Candy*.

After setting up a charity dedicated to helping the children of Malawi, Madonna wanted to raise awareness of just what life for the African orphans was really like. In 2008 she released *I Am Because We Are*, a documentary dedicated to this cause, telling the stories of various families in the country and taking the viewer on a journey into their lives. Madonna asked her assistant/gardener Nathan Rissman if he would like to work with her on the project, and he was more than happy to do it. Together they began, with Madonna writing, producing and also narrating, while

Rissman took on the job of directing.

At first Madonna preferred to take a back seat while telling the story of the orphans, but filmmaker Michael Moore encouraged the singer to tell her story too. She did, and the result is a personal and at times devastating look at the ravaged country.

This photo shows Madonna with Michael Moore, at the Traverse City Film Festival in August 2008, where she screened *I Am Because We Are*. Her father and step-mother can be seen behind them, chatting to granddaughter Lourdes.

By the time September 2008 rolled around, rumours were rife that Madonna and Guy Ritchie were about to separate for good. These rumours were cemented during the couple's appearance at the premiere of Ritchie's new movie, *RocknRolla*, where they were seen looking obviously uncomfortable in each other's company.

During a press conference for the film, reporters tried to quiz Ritchie about the state of the relationship, as well as the publication of Christopher Ciccone's book, *Life with My Sister Madonna*. Ritchie managed to avoid answering each question, but by October 2008, while Madonna was on her *Sticky & Sweet* tour, the news was official – the marriage was over and divorce proceedings were about to begin.

The details of the separation were, for the most part, kept under wraps, although it was revealed by Madonna's spokesperson that Guy got to keep the country mansion. Madonna, meanwhile, kept the London townhouse, where she still resides when in England. Since then the two have been photographed together on several occasions, including shortly after the divorce when he met her to pick up his sons, and then during Rocco's bar mitzvah celebration in 2013, at a New York parkour centre.

Madonna's next tour, *Sticky & Sweet*, kicked off in Cardiff in August 2008 and continued until December, where it ended in São Paulo, Brazil. However, Madonna then did something she had never done before and announced that the tour would be extended, kicking off again in London during July 2009 and going through to September, where it finally ended in Tel Aviv, Israel.

The tour was a controversial one for several reasons, including the fact that Madonna's marriage broke up during it, and then because of the political statements that she continued to put into her concert speeches. Then, during the 2009 leg of the tour, tragedy struck when the stage collapsed, injuring eight workers and killing two. The concert was understandably cancelled that evening and Madonna went to visit not only the surviving crew members, but also the families of everyone involved, releasing a statement to say that she was "devastated" and offering her prayers and deepest sympathy.

This photo shows Madonna during the Gypsy section of the show, at Madison Square Garden, New York.

Away from the controversies and tragedies, the show itself was a mixture of old and new songs, with some differing when the show continued during 2009. Much of it came from her *Hard Candy* album, but there were classics too, such as "Human Nature", "Vogue" and "La Isla Bonita".

At times it seemed as though barbed comments were being aimed at estranged husband Guy Ritchie, particularly during "Miles Away" and a new version of "Borderline". At other times, pictures of famine and global warming were projected on the screen. However, by the end of the show, the feeling was more upbeat, and Madonna encouraged audience participation by asking them to suggest "an oldie but goodie" for her to sing. A brief rendition of the chosen song would be followed by "Hung Up" and then the final song, "Give It 2 Me". Throughout the concert, video backdrops included clips of Kanye West, Britney Spears, Pharrell Williams and Justin Timberlake, and at times during the tour, some of the backdrop stars did make a special appearance in person.

This photo shows Madonna skipping at Madison Square Garden, New York.

Filth and Wisdom was premiered in February 2008 at the Berlin Film Festival, and then received a slightly more glamorous screening in New York in October of that year. Although Madonna and Guy had separated by the time of the second screening, there had been no official announcement yet, and reporters were eager to ask the new director about her husband. To her credit, Madonna did not bite or give any time to the probing questions, and instead explained that she had received some guidance from Guy about how to direct a movie. His biggest piece of advice, she said, was to show up to the set with confidence even if she felt nervous or unsure.

Unfortunately, while Madonna may have looked fabulous at the premiere, the same cannot be said for the reviews of *Filth and Wisdom*. The critics believed that the singer could not direct actors, and did not hold back from sharing their views with the world.

This photo shows Madonna at the New York premiere, with the other Guy in her life – manager Guy Oseary – whom she has worked with for a great many years.

Madonna is, was and always will be a huge advocate of keeping fit and toning her body. She has tried many different fitness techniques over the years, including biking, jogging, weights, yoga and Pilates, with a variety of trainers, but perhaps one of her most famous is Tracy Anderson. For a time in the late 2000s, Madonna was seen frequently with Anderson, walking to and from her gym, which was located next to her London home. The two were thought to be inseparable, but this all changed in 2009 when Madonna decided to let Anderson go.

The media reported that the decision was because the trainer had become friendly with Philippe van den Bossche, the former head of Madonna's Raising Malawi charity, but this was something Madonna later denied. "I wanted to try something different," she told reporters, before adding that she wished Anderson and van den Bossche well. Since then she has gone onto hire a new trainer – Nicole Winhoffer – and the two have released several keep-fit DVDs based on Madonna's routines, as well as working together on the launch of Hard Candy Fitness clubs. Anderson, meanwhile, continues to train celebrities such as Gwyneth Paltrow and has also released a DVD.

This photo shows Madonna and Tracy Anderson in 2008, walking home after a workout.

Madonna may have come in for much criticism after the adoption of David Banda, but the condemnation did not stop her from wanting to adopt another child from Malawi – this time a little girl called Mercy. However, when she visited the country in March 2009 to make her plans official, the courts stood in her way, citing the fact that the singer did not reside there as a way of preventing the adoption. Madonna was forced to return home without the child, but vowed to fight in order to overturn the ruling.

Though the trip may have been a disappointment in many ways, it did give Madonna the chance to reunite her son David with his natural father, Yohane Banda, who later told reporters: "Madonna found David frail and sickly but I couldn't believe my eyes how he had been transformed when I met him in March." He then went on to describe how the boy was "big and bouncy" and that he felt extremely happy for him. Banda also gave his support in the adoption of Mercy, saying that the singer should be allowed to adopt the child; that it would be good for her in the long run.

This photo shows Madonna and her family visiting an orphanage in Malawi, as she waited to hear if the adoption of Mercy would be permitted.

In June 2009, several months after the initial ruling to stop Madonna's adoption of Mercy, the Supreme Court overturned the decision and allowed the singer to take the child home to New York. Madonna was ecstatic and released a statement saying that she and her family looked forward to sharing their lives with her.

Since then Mercy seems to have fitted into the family with no trouble whatsoever. The little girl travels everywhere with her mother, who often shares photos of Mercy and her brother, David, on her Instagram and Facebook accounts. The singer posts such events as Easter egg hunts, playing in the garden, horse riding and even meeting superstar Beyonce. Photos of the young girl are often seen in the newspapers, where she is seen waving happily to reporters, dressing up in pretty dresses and skipping along the street.

This photo shows Mercy and Madonna during a trip to Paris in July 2009, just weeks after her arrival into the family.

The first love interest in Madonna's life after the breakdown of her marriage to Guy Ritchie came in the shape of Jesus Luz, a Brazilian model who was nearly thirty years her junior. The two met when Steven Klein hired Luz to work with Madonna during a photo shoot for *W* magazine in December 2008, and they became romantically linked from then on. The first time they were officially photographed together was at the beginning of 2009, but by the time this photo was taken, at a party in September of that year, they had been an item for some time, and seemed to be comfortable in each other's company.

Despite the age difference, for a while the couple seemed to be a good fit, and he was seen frequently spending time not only with Madonna, but her children too. He also began studying the Kabbalah, something which he later said had been introduced to him by his girlfriend and had given him a way of being strong. In the summer of 2009, Luz was cast opposite Madonna in the video for her new single, "Celebration": an upbeat song released from the compilation album of the same name.

When Lady Gaga appeared on the music scene, she and Madonna seemed to get along quite well, but over the years cracks have begun to appear between the two. During a 2009 episode of *Saturday Night Live*, they took part in a skit which showed them fighting. The scene was supposed to be comedic, of course, but the chemistry between the two was almost non-existent and the whole thing ended up awkward and somewhat bizarre.

When Gaga released the single "Born This Way" in 2011, it was felt by some that the song bore a striking resemblance to Madonna's 1989 hit "Express Yourself". In 2012, Madonna made her feelings clear when she called the incident "reductive", and then added more during the *MDNA* tour by singing a mash-up of "Born This Way", "Express Yourself" and "She's Not Me".

This photo from 2009 shows the two singers when they appeared to get along quite well.

2009 was a busy year for Madonna and her association with Malawi, and in October she made a trip to talk about the first stages of construction on a new girls' school. She accompanied the visit with a video for her fans, explaining that since being introduced to the plight of Malawi children some seven years ago, it had taken over her life. "I am so grateful that it has," she said. In the video, the singer also spoke about her charity, Raising Malawi, and how she was working to get many projects off the ground, including the school.

The video ended with Madonna asking for people to help with fundraising, and promised that for every dollar donated, she would match it. "That's very important to me," she said, before thanking everyone for their support.

This photo shows the singer planting a tree during her October trip, in order to officially launch the girls' academy project in Lilongwe.

In late 2009, Madonna was assigned to star in a series of adverts for designers Dolce & Gabbana, which were then released in 2010 along with a collection of sunglasses designed by the singer herself. She had been a fan of their clothes for many years, so to work with them on the project was no doubt something the singer didn't have to think about for very long. Meanwhile, the designers themselves said that it was all a dream come true.

In the black-and-white campaign photos, Madonna is seen being incredibly domesticated: preparing dinner, holding a broom in her hand, spending time with a fictional family and doing the washing up. The photos gave the feel of an Italian mother living her life, and the fun had on the Steven Klein shoot was clear when footage was released showing her laughingly scrubbing the floor and dealing with escaped chickens.

This photo shows Madonna with Stefano Gabbana (left) and Domenico Dolce, at the Gold club in Milan, Italy, shortly before working on the campaign.

At the beginning of 2010, it was reported that Madonna and Jesus Luz were looking to get married, but then very shortly afterwards rumours circulated that they had actually called the relationship off. The reason, according to "friends", was that Jesus in particular felt they had nothing in common any more. However, several days after the initial reports broke, Madonna and Jesus were spotted with Madonna's children at the Rio de Janeiro Carnival, though while the singer seemed relaxed and joyful to be there, he seemed less so. Photographs of the event (such as this one) show the model looking fairly fed up, as his girlfriend smiles happily beside him.

By the time they returned to the United States, the romance had most definitely fizzled out. The pair went their separate ways and Jesus has continued with his modelling career, as well as doing a stint on Italy's version of *Dancing with the Stars*.

Madonna has worked with photographer Steven Klein on many occasions, including photo shoots for *W* magazine and backdrop videos shown on stage when she is changing costume. In 2003 the pair teamed up to create an art exhibition entitled *X-STaTIC PRO=CeSS* which included photos and footage of Madonna contorting herself into various yoga/acrobatic poses. The piece was accompanied by a haunting musical score that included the song "The Beast Within".

Fans have had a mixed reaction to the exhibition – which today can be viewed on the Internet – with some declaring it a fantastic piece of art, while others brand it creepy and cold. But despite the mixed reaction, Klein and Madonna have gone on to collaborate on many other occasions and obviously enjoy each other's work.

This photo shows the two friends (centre) at a reception hosted by Moet & Chandon in Los Angeles, March 2010.

April 2010 saw Madonna travel once again to Malawi, with her children. Whilst there, she visited orphanages and children's centres, as well as the site of what she hoped would be the Academy for Girls, built with money she had raised over the past few years. Once there, the singer placed a brick to signify the beginning of official construction. She also helped feed farm animals, before trying her hand at various pieces of equipment such as the water pump that can be seen in this photo.

Ultimately, the girls' academy Madonna was planning to build did not go ahead, after a shake-up of the management committee. Instead the singer invested money into funding a number of community schools which would educate and nurture both boys and girls. This decision did not go down well with certain members of the Malawi government, however, who criticised the star's change of mind and declared her charitable involvement with the country as over.

For a long time Madonna has been interested in the romance between Wallace Simpson and Edward Windsor. In 2009 she announced that she had written a script, entitled *W.E.* with friend Alek Keshishian, and it began shooting – to much fanfare – in summer 2010. The movie revolved around the story of the Duke and Duchess, as well as a modern-day woman called Wally Winthrop who is obsessed with the idea of their "perfect love". It was a huge undertaking, and Madonna worked tirelessly on all aspects of the production, including doing lots of research. However, with shooting locations in the UK, France and New York, as well as a story taking in a variety of different times and eras, she later summed up the experience as "a bloody nightmare" and a huge challenge.

The cast appreciated what their director was trying to do, and she helped them as much as she could, by sending over boxes of books and DVDs to help their own research. As well as that, she would send emails at all times of the day and night, leading one of the actors to comment that she mustn't have had any time to sleep at all.

This photo shows Madonna on the New York film set.

When researching and shooting her film *W.E.*, Madonna was determined that she would have access to as many Wallace- and Edward-related items as she could find. With this in mind, she contacted Muhammad Al Fayed, who not only owned a lot of letters, but also the Duke and Duchess's Paris home.

When Madonna first approached Al Fayed to gain permission to use the items in her research, the two worked out a fair trade situation, in that he would allow her request if he approved the script and she did something for him in return. The favour asked of Madonna was to visit Kent's West Heath school for children with emotional or communication difficulties. She jumped at the chance, and appeared at a fundraiser in June 2010.

By the time it was released, *W.E.* received some incredibly negative reviews, possibly – and unfairly – because of the person directing it. While it is certainly not to everyone's taste, *W.E.* is a beautifully shot movie and, bearing in mind that this was Madonna's first feature-length film, the direction is superb.

This photo shows Madonna with Andrea Riseborough, who played Wallace Simpson.

Madonna

For thirty years, Madonna has been known as the "Material Girl", so when her daughter, Lourdes, expressed an interest in working with her on a fashion line, it made good sense to call it after the moniker. During the creation of Material Girl, the two took part in design meetings, and Madonna admitted that for the most part it was teenager Lourdes creating the looks, while she offered quiet support in the background.

In September 2010 the range was launched, and mother and daughter took to the red (or pink in this case) carpet at New York store Macy's to discuss their work. During the event, Madonna gave a speech and said that, while she has achieved a lot of things in her lifetime, watching her daughter work on the fashion line and make her dreams come true was the most exciting thing she had ever done.

Since then, the fashion line has gone from strength to strength, and Lourdes and Madonna have promoted the range in many ways, including a tongue-in-cheek video showing the two playfully arguing about what it means to be a "Material Girl".

This photo shows mother and daughter on their arrival at Macy's.

Well and truly inspired by *W.E.*, Madonna arrived at the 2011 Met Ball in a glorious Stella McCartney outfit, which was blue with silver stars cascading down the back. Her long hair was curled and worn over her shoulders, while in her hand she carried a small silver purse. However, while the assorted fans and media thought she looked stunning, the star herself surprisingly said she felt rather fat. This, of course, led to a barrage of column inches berating the toned star for daring to say such a thing about herself.

What didn't prove controversial, however, were her thoughts on late designer Alexander McQueen, who had passed away in 2010. Madonna told reporters that she missed him terribly, both as a designer and a friend, and that the industry was a duller place without him. "I hope he's having fun wherever he is right now," she added.

This photo shows Madonna on the red carpet, in the famous Stella McCartney gown.

The publicity for Madonna's film *W.E.* was long and involved a great many appearances at film festivals and scheduled premieres. During each one she would pose with members of the cast and often speak to the audience about her love for the movie. There were a number of press conferences too, and while all make interesting viewing, perhaps the one that caused the most sensation came in September 2011 during the Venice Film Festival, when a fan presented her with a huge hydrangea. She thanked him, put it under the desk and then leant over to actress Andrea Riseborough, exclaiming that she "absolutely loathed" hydrangeas.

Unfortunately for her, the microphone picked up every word, and the story was beamed around the world, with some critics slamming Madonna for her lack of respect towards the fan involved. However, the "fan" was actually Vitalii Sediuk, a serial prankster who likes to create chaos on stages and red carpets around the world. Indeed, in 2014 he even crawled under the dress of actress America Ferrera during the Cannes Film Festival.

Madonna later released a funny silent movie in response to all the criticism surrounding the hydrangea episode, expressing how sorry she was for causing the flowers hurt and pain. It ended in true Madonna style, with the star declaring that she really did hate hydrangeas before throwing them on the floor and expressing her love for roses instead.

This photo shows Madonna and *W.E.* cast members at the Venice Film Festival.

Madonna won a Golden Globe for *Evita* in 1996, but in 2012 she was back for a totally different reason – winning the award for Best Original Song for "Masterpiece", taken from the *W.E.* soundtrack.

Dressed in an elegant silver gown, with her hair flowing past her shoulders, Madonna accepted her award very humbly and told the audience that it had come as a great surprise. She thanked her co-writers, her manager Guy Oseary and the other people involved in the film, and became so caught up in the moment that the music started to play in order to remind her to leave the stage.

Once the Globes were out of the way, speculation mounted that "Masterpiece" would earn an Oscar win for Madonna, but it was not to be. Just as she was snubbed in 1997 for *Evita*, so it was that the Academy failed to give her even a nomination for *W.E.* Instead the Oscar for best song went to "Man or Muppet", from *The Muppet Movie*.

In February 2012, just before her appearance at the Super Bowl half-time show, Madonna took part in a press conference to talk about the upcoming show. During the event she explained that throughout her entire career, she had never worked so hard, nor been so "freaked out" as she had been when trying to organise the Super Bowl show. The singer also revealed that she would be dedicating the performance to her father because of the work ethic he had instilled in her, and explained that if she never stopped working, it was because of his influence. "I'm sure out of all the things I've ever done in my life, this will be the thing he's most excited about," she said.

The conference was a very informal affair, and involved questions about possible wardrobe malfunctions and whether she would like to be a judge on *The X Factor*. Madonna answered all with good humour and then topped it off with a demonstration of how she practises salsa moves, which can be seen in this photograph.

The appearance of Madonna at the 2012 Super Bowl half-time show was the most watched in the event's history. The singer was carried across the stadium on a huge, gold throne, surrounded by 150 burly men. After which she took to the stage and launched into an energetic rendition of "Vogue" with her dancers. Next came "Music", which saw her dancing and doing acrobatics, while a man slack lined in front of her, and then LMFAO joined her to sing a few bars of "Sexy and I Know It".

The most controversial part of the evening included the forthcoming single, "Gimme All Your Luvin", which involved singers M.I.A. and Nicki Minaj. During the song, M.I.A. gave the middle finger to the audience, which caused uproar around the USA and was still being complained about some two years later.

Cee Lo Green joined her next, this time for an "Open Your Heart/Express Yourself" medley, before launching into an extremely emotional rendition of "Like a Prayer", as can be seen in this photo. Madonna later said that the intensity of this part of the show almost brought her to tears.

Madonna's next album was entitled *MDNA* and was released in March 2012. Teaming up once again with William Orbit, as well as various other producers, the album was the first to be created under her new contract with Live Nation/Interscope. The album caused some controversy due to its provocative title, which many claimed sounded too close to the drug MDMA. Madonna herself said that it was chosen because it is a shortened version of her own name, but the similarities were certainly a talking point during early 2012.

For many fans, *MDNA* was a much better album than *Hard Candy*, and it was clear that the singer was exorcising a lot of the anger towards her marriage break-up in some of the songs. One of the bonus tracks in particular – entitled "I Fucked Up" – seemed to point the finger of blame firmly towards herself, while others, such as "I Don't Give A", looked as though the guilt was being placed elsewhere.

While the album shot to the top of the charts as soon as it was released, it quickly fell, thanks mainly to Madonna's limited promotion and the fact that she did very few interviews. Instead it was mainly publicised on Facebook and other social networking sites, including with a live-stream chat between her and interviewer Jimmy Fallon, which can be seen in this photo.

Madonna had been approached to create her own perfume for a number of years, but had always stalled in actually releasing one she felt would be a worthy contribution. That changed in April 2012 when she launched a scent entitled – quite appropriately – Truth or Dare, after the documentary of the same name. During publicity for the fragrance, Madonna explained that she wanted it to smell like her mother, and so therefore created a smell that had a heavy floral base with lots of gardenia.

The launch of the perfume included an elaborate advertising campaign, as well as an appearance at Macy's, where the singer signed her name on the arm of an admirer. He then went straight out to get the ink permanently tattooed.

In late 2012, Madonna released another fragrance entitled Truth or Dare: Naked, which shared the same basic bottle design but with subtle differences. The actual perfume was very different, however, and this time included such notes as honeysuckle, vanilla orchid, cocoa flower and cedar wood.

Madonna's 2012 concert tour was *MDNA*, and she travelled the world from May to December 2012. Out of all the tours she has done, it was perhaps this one that was the most audience-friendly, with many people getting up close and personal, shaking the star's hand and singing with her. As she had done during *Sticky & Sweet*, Madonna also thrilled fans by allowing some into soundchecks before the concert, chatting to them, making jokes and singing songs.

Boasting an impressive twenty-four tracks (including musical interludes), the *MDNA* show was described by Madonna as being a journey from darkness to light. With this in mind, the beginning of the show was much talked about when it depicted gun violence, which resulted in some critics requesting she remove it. Madonna refused to do any such thing, and in echoes of the stop-over in Toronto during the *Blond Ambition* tour where she was threatened with arrest over the masturbation scene, the singer claimed she would rather cancel than change the show.

But while the first part of the show was controversial, by the time "Express Yourself" was performed, the show had proceeded to another, more upbeat section, with a cheerleading theme. This part of the concert came complete with pompoms and full costumes, all of which can be seen in this photo.

"Human Nature", which showed Madonna stripping off her outfit to reveal skimpy underwear and fishnet stockings, was shocking for some people, but things went further during several of the concerts on the tour, when the singer chose to use this section to flash one of her breasts to the crowd. The media went crazy, with many detractors saying she should never have done such a thing. The outrage only caused headlines and publicity for the tour, however, which could never be a bad thing as far as Madonna was concerned.

"Like a Virgin" was performed in the shape of a ballad, while "Like a Prayer" was a crowd-pleaser as ever, complete with gongs, bells and audience participation when Madonna encouraged some of the fans to sing into her microphone. By the time the end of the show came, it was a full-on celebration, both in terms of mood and song, when everything transformed into a giant disco complete with DJ booths that appeared out of the stage. Madonna always appeared elated by this point, and an example of that can be seen in this photo, showing the happy singer balanced on the shoulders of one of her dancers.

While Madonna's children have often made small appearances on stage and in the audience of her shows, she was thrilled when son Rocco told her he wanted to be involved in a more creative way during *MDNA*. The twelve-year-old always had an interest in entertaining, so when he first informed his mother that he wanted to dance, she was more than willing to let him give it a go. At first Rocco was involved in a very small way, but as rehearsals gained momentum, so too did his enthusiasm, and by the time the *MDNA* tour hit the road, the young dancer was included in several songs, including "Open Your Heart" and "Celebration". He also appeared as a member of the choir during "Like a Prayer".

In October 2012, the tour reached Los Angeles and Madonna paid a visit to *The Ellen Show*, where Rocco appeared again, this time sitting in a glass tank in order to be "gunked" for charity.

This photo shows Madonna and Rocco on stage at Madison Square Garden, singing "Open Your Heart".

Shortly after splitting with Jesus Luz, Madonna met dancer Brahim Zaibat, who was thirty years her junior. The two began dating, and the media were quick to pick up on the fact that, as with Luz, Madonna was older than her boyfriend's mother. On the fascination surrounding the relationship, the singer claimed it to be a "boring old chestnut" and added that dating a younger man was not something she had ever gone out to do intentionally; it was just something that had occurred because she got along with Zaibat, regardless of age.

The two spent a lot of time together during the *MDNA* tour, when Zaibat was a backing dancer for the show. They then continued to be seen together after the tour ended, though by the end of 2013 the couple had broken up. Madonna's publicist assured reporters that the two had just grown apart, though some speculated that the reason had something to do with Zaibat's participation in the French version of *Dancing with the Stars*, which had kept them from being together.

This photo shows the couple together in Rome, during the *MDNA* tour.

When Madonna was invited to present TV personality Anderson Cooper with the Vito Russo Award at the GLAAD (Gay and Lesbian Alliance Against Defamation) Awards, she took to the stage wearing a Boy Scout uniform, complete with shorts, badges and hat. In her speech she told the audience that she had wanted to become a Boy Scout but they wouldn't let her join. "I think that's fucked up," she said, before adding that she knew how to make fires and pitch a tent, had an excellent sense of direction and, what's more, knew how to scout for boys, jokingly referring to her penchant for younger men.

While the first part of the speech was slightly tongue-in-cheek, it did have a lot of truth in it, especially when Madonna declared that the rules were stupid and should be changed. Always an advocate for equal rights, she then went on to tell the audience that bullying, bigotry and discrimination seemed to be a manifestation of the unknown, and that hearing about young people who killed themselves because of these things made her want to "cry a river of tears". The whole speech was thought-provoking, and the ultimate message was that if only people could look under the surface, they would see that everyone is not so different after all.

This photo shows Madonna giving her speech in the Boy Scout uniform.

Whilst her charity Raising Malawi had been under some scrutiny in the press for alleged mismanagement in the country itself, Madonna continued her support of the nation. In April 2013 she travelled there once again in order to visit orphanages, centres and the schools she was helping to build and renovate.

Accompanied by her children, the singer held a press conference to say how happy she was to be back, how welcome she felt, and that she was there because she felt deeply about the children of Malawi. "Regardless of the challenges, the ups and downs . . . I have not forgotten my commitment to the children," she said, before adding that her goal was to continue the work she had been doing, particularly in education and healthcare.

All seemed well until Malawi's president, Joyce Banda, was said to have complained about Madonna's trip, citing her need to "generate recognition" and receive special treatment. It was also claimed that the schools Madonna had opened were just blocks attached to existing establishments. The singer immediately put out a statement saying she had never asked for special treatment, and that she was saddened by the stories regarding what they had accomplished, reiterating that her intention would always be in helping the children. Finally, the matter ended when it was claimed the president herself had not said those things; they were put out without her permission, and she was furious about it.

This photo shows Madonna, David and Mercy meeting the Executive Director of the Mphandula Childrencare Centre during their visit.

While Madonna's appearance at the 2011 Met Ball was glamour personified, she was the complete opposite during the May 2013 event, when patrons were encouraged to "go Punk". The singer arrived with then-boyfriend Braham Zaibat and was dressed in a fishnet outfit complete with studded checked jacket, chains and severe black wig. While talking to interviewers on the red carpet, Madonna explained that she loved the Sid Vicious/Nancy Spungen era, so decided to go with that theme, but put her own twist on it at the same time.

Photographers went wild at the sight of such an outfit, and Madonna's press rep Liz Rosenberg was seen directing proceedings as she made her way down the red carpet, telling the singer where to turn and moving her boyfriend out of shot when the time required.

This photo shows Madonna with property developer Andre Balazs (left) and fashion designer Riccardo Tisci, inside the event.

Chime for Change is a campaign to raise funds and awareness in the promotion of education, health and justice for girls and women. These are causes close to Madonna's heart, so when the organisation announced their intention to put on a concert – The Sound of Change – the singer did not have to think twice about offering her services as a speaker.

Held in June 2013 at Twickenham Stadium, London, the concert was extremely popular. Madonna's speech was both inspiring and informative, describing women who are risking their lives in the name of empowering women as "Brave Warriors", and introducing two such ladies to the stage. Afterwards, she told a backstage reporter that she wanted to be part of the event because she had been focused on building schools for children in recent years, and therefore the event and her passion seemed to be a perfect fit. "We need more people willing to fight the fight," she explained.

This photo shows Madonna during her speech.

Madonna has been a fan of designer Stella McCartney since the very beginning of her career and the two have been close friends since the singer moved to England in the late 1990s. They have been spotted together frequently, at parties, award ceremonies and out on the town, and the singer even tried to introduce Stella to the teachings of Kabbalah, though the designer has been quick to admit she didn't really understand it.

The friendship has seen some highs and lows – the highest probably when Stella acted as a bridesmaid for Madonna in 2000 – and the lowest most likely when Madonna was seen wearing fur and shooting pheasants, much to the vegetarian designer's chagrin.

This photo shows Madonna and Stella in June 2013, at a spring presentation in New York. The hug they shared after the event shows that any ups and downs over the years have done nothing to diminish their close friendship.

In June 2013 the film version of the
MDNA tour was premiered in New
York. Dressed in a Marlene Dietrich-
style outfit, Madonna thanked
her dancers, crew members and
managers, while talking candidly to
her fans about her time on tour. Some
of the fans ("Triangle Bitches", as
Madonna jokingly called them, thanks
to the fact that they were forever in
the triangle section of the auditorium)
had literally travelled around the
world with the tour, and asked many
questions about what life was like

on the road. One admirer, whom
Madonna knew by name, thanked her
for what he described as the best year
of his life, while another told the star
that he'd been a fan for thirty years,
since he was just seven years old.

Madonna's casual and happy
interaction with her fans, both during
the *MDNA* tour and on Facebook, has
shown a new side to the woman who
in the past seemed to distance herself
from social media and fan interaction.
This photo shows the singer enjoying
her time at the *MDNA* event.

In late summer 2013, Madonna started to hint that she had another project in the works, or a "secret project" to be more precise. Finally, in September it was a mystery no more, when the star released a short film entitled *secretprojectrevolution* along with an exclusive interview with Eddy Moretti from Vice, a company that was involved in the project.

The black-and-white film, directed by Madonna and her friend Steven Klein, was inspired by various examples of oppression, which the star had seen during her time on the road with the *MDNA* tour. It had bothered her that people seemed to be becoming less tolerant of others, and through various scenes showing violence, discrimination, dance and expression, the film encouraged people to be more tolerant of each other, and to start a revolution of love.

At the same time, the film launched the Art for Freedom project, a medium to encourage people to express what freedom means to them, through film, music, poetry and photography. This photo shows Madonna at the *secretprojectrevolution* premiere in New York, which saw her taking to the stage with son Rocco in order to express themselves through a mixture of song and dance.

In 2010, Madonna embarked on a new project, this time opening a series of centres called Hard Candy Fitness. The first was opened in Mexico during November 2010, with others following in countries around the world. The aim was to allow patrons to share the workouts that Madonna herself does with trainer Nicole Winhoffer, and from the start they proved popular with fans of both the singer and all-round fitness.

During publicity for the new venture, Madonna has been candid with her thoughts on her own health, describing how over the years she has enjoyed a number of forms of exercise and has now come to the point where she has been able to develop a system that encompasses everything she loves to do. "I need to do it at least five times a week, or I start to get depressed," she told reporters during the opening of Hard Candy Fitness in Berlin.

This photo shows Madonna arriving at the opening of the German centre, in October 2013.

In November 2013, Madonna lent her support to ex-husband Sean Penn by flying down to Haiti with her son Rocco in order to see the work he had been doing with the J/P Haitian Relief Organization. For several days Madonna shared various photos of the trip, including one of her and Sean together, while Rocco posted one of him sharing a car with the actor, captioned "trouble is always here".

While the trip was very much about helping the charity, the media of course were more concerned with the fact that Sean seemed to be spending so much time with his ex-wife. The flames were fanned by his earlier appearance at the *secretprojectrevolution* screening, where the two were photographed hugging and posing for the cameras. Rumours abounded that the couple were going to spend Thanksgiving together and were on the verge of reconciliation, but this was ultimately proved false when Sean began a much-publicised relationship with actress Charlize Theron.

This photo shows Madonna at Los Angeles Airport, in preparation for her trip to Haiti.

In January 2014, Madonna arrived at the Grammy Awards on the arm of her son, David, both wearing matching "gangster" outfits. The two were a hit on the red carpet, and when asked if he had styled his mother that evening, the youngster declared that he had indeed. David showed great confidence in the spotlight, telling the interviewer that, whilst his mother was wearing a grill on her teeth, he was not, even though she had promised that he could have one for his eighth birthday. Madonna seemed a little taken aback, and assured the youngster that they just hadn't had time to get his mouth measured by the dentist yet. (Several weeks later she posted a photo of the youngster on Facebook, with his very own grill in place.)

A more serious part of the proceedings came later in the evening, when Macklemore, Mary Lambert and Ryan Lewis sang "Same Love" on stage, while Queen Latifah officiated over the marriage of thirty-three couples in the audience, consisting of same sex, transgender and heterosexual couples. That done, Madonna appeared dressed all in white, and began a slowed-down version of her 1986 classic "Open Your Heart", while the newly married couples all walked down the aisle.

This photograph shows Madonna and David posing for the press in attendance that evening.

Miley Cyrus became famous for her role in the Disney TV series *Hannah Montana*, but in recent years she has been better known for her "twerking" performance at the 2013 MTV awards with Robin Thicke. In late January 2014, the singer recorded an *Unplugged* special, and invited Madonna along to sing a duet with her.

Dressed in cowboy gear, the two sang and danced along to Madonna's "Don't Tell Me", before launching into Miley's hit "We Can't Stop". The two songs fitted very well together and at one point were being performed simultaneously by both singers. The appearance caused some controversy, with various viewers calling the provocative dance moves too much for television. However, compared to many other things seen in modern-day pop videos, the performance was nothing much to complain about.

This photo shows the two singers during publicity for the event, dressed in the same costumes they had worn on stage.

When Madonna's *MDNA* tour reached Russia in 2012, the group Pussy Riot were being put on trial for singing a song which criticised the government. The singer was appalled and from that moment, she spoke freely in her support of Pussy Riot during her concerts. Immediately, Madonna found herself receiving a number of threats and abuse for her support not only of the women in the group, but also of gay rights. However – and quite rightly – no threats will ever stop the star from speaking her mind and defending people and subjects she feels strongly about.

Two years later, in February 2014, Madonna appeared at the Amnesty International Benefit Concert to speak about her experiences and beliefs and to describe how lucky she felt to live in a country that enabled freedom of speech. Once she had completed her talk, the singer introduced two members of Pussy Riot, and embraced them on stage.

This photo shows Madonna making her impassioned speech at the concert.

In early 2014, Madonna was spotted around New York, hobbling into her house with the aid of crutches. It was announced to the press that the singer had bruised a bone in her foot while dancing in high heels, but that the problem wasn't serious and she expected to recover in a short time.

As with most things, the bruised foot was not enough to keep Madonna from the gym, and she was photographed leaving her local establishment, complete with dark glasses and a scarf around her face, crutches in hand. As time went on, the singer was spotted at other public appearances, such as the Great American Songbook event held to honour talent agent Bryan Lourd. This photograph shows Madonna at the February 2014 event, complete with sensible shoes and black cane.